The World As Creation

Creation in Christ
in an Evolutionary World View

D1496342

Zacchaeus Studies: Theology

General Editor: Monika Hellwig

The World As Creation

Creation in Christ
in an Evolutionary World View

by

Emily Binns

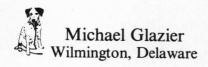

Michael Glazier
Wilmington, Delaware

About the Author

Emily Binns is a professor of systematic theology at Villanova University, Villanova, Pa. She is one of the world's foremost authorities on Teilhard de Chardin and his influence, and her scholarly articles have appeared in *The Teilhard Review, The American Ecclesiastical Review, Liturgy,* and *Union Theological Review.* Professor Binns was the first woman to deliver the prestigious *Thomas More Lectures* at Yale University.

First published in 1990 by Michael Glazier, Inc., 1935 West Fourth Street, Wilmington, Delaware 19805.

Library of Congress Cataloging-in-Publication Data

Binns, Emily
   The world as creation: creation in Christ in an evolutionary world view/by Emily Binns.

    p. cm.—(Zacchaeus studies. Theology)
   Includes bibliographical references.
   ISBN 0-89453-755-5
   1. Creation. 2. Evolution—Religious aspects—Christianity.
  I. Title. II. Series.
  BT695.B48   1990
  231.7'65—dc20   89-78382
                                            CIP

Cover Design by Maureen Daney
Typography by Cyndi Cohee
Printed in the United States by St. Mary's

TABLE OF CONTENTS

4. The Word and Hope:
    The Christological Dimension 74

Conclusion: Towards a Contemporary
    Creation Spirituality 80

Bibliography 88
Appendices 92
Index 101

*For Amy and Jimmie,
and all the children of the world
with the firm hope that their world
will become one of ever-increasing
consciousness, so that peace
and justice may be the way
of their future.*

Acknowledgments

I would like to express my gratitude to all who have helped to bring this project to completion: most especially, to Dr. Monika K. Hellwig, Georgetown University, who initially suggested the book and continued to encourage me; to Eugene L. Tucker, S.J., and Michael Crosby, O.F.M., Cap., for reading the manuscript and carefully criticizing it throughout; to Susan Woehlke and Tom Steyaert, competent graduate assistants, for their able completion of a variety of essential tasks; to Martin Connell for his careful preparation of the manuscript; and to my students whose questions have continued to prompt me to further explorations.

We have been urged, as theologians, to grasp the centrality and importance of understanding Creation in a new key, and I hope that this effort will be fruitful for all those readers hoping to understand more about our amazing universe, in its continuous process of development. Pierre Teilhard de Chardin, S.J., whose luminous thought underlies much of what is written here, dedicated his *Divine Milieu* "to those who love the earth." I can do no better than to thank him and do likewise.

Editor's Note

This series of short texts in doctrinal subjects is designed to offer introductory volumes accessible to any educated reader. Dealing with the central topics of Christian faith, the authors have set out to explain the theological interpretation of these topics in a Catholic context without assuming a professional theological training on the part of the reader.

We who have worked on the series hope that these books will serve well in college theology classes where they can be used either as a series or as individual introductory presentations leading to a deeper exploration of a particular topic. We also hope that these books will be widely used and useful in adult study circles, continuing education and RENEW programs, and will be picked up by casual browsers in bookstores. We want to serve the needs of any who are trying to understand more thoroughly the meaning of the Catholic faith and its relevance to the changing circumstances of our times.

Each author has endeavored to present the biblical foundation, the traditional development, the official church position and the contemporary theological discussion of the doctrine or topic in hand. Controversial questions are discussed within the context of the established teaching and the accepted theological interpretation.

We undertook the series in response to increasing interest among educated Catholics in issues arising in the contemporary church, doctrines that raise new questions in a contemporary setting, and teachings that now call for wider and deeper appreciation. To such people we offer these volumes, hoping that reading them may be a satisfying and heartening experience.

Monika K. Hellwig
Series Editor

Introduction

The present state of the question regarding the understanding of creation as process and the concept of a dynamic universe constantly changing and developing, has been with us challenging us, for more than a century. No single concept has exerted more influence on theological thought than the gradual internalization of this understanding of the World as an ongoing Creation. Ideas about God, human relationship with God, the problem of evil, the diminishment of evil, and the meaning of spirituality and eschatology all shift in the face of the awesome dimensions of evolution, of unfinished process.

From the earliest time that human persons could reflect on their own existence, and become aware of the self and of the other, questions about the why and how of created reality have abounded and have received multiple responses through all world religions.

The carefully constructed Hebrew story recounted in Genesis served as a viable understanding in the West just so long as the world continued to be seen as a fixed reality, finished in some long distant past. Correspondingly, the questions about evil and its origins found resolution in a single human act also lodged deep in the past.

With the blossoming of Christianity out of its Jewish roots, the meaning and significance of Jesus the Christ was expressed in terms of redemption of that "once perfect, now flawed" Creation. The Incarnation, the entrance of divinity into human flesh and history, was seen as a remedial "after-thought" to that Creation. No matter that the Prologue of John's Gospel and the letters of Paul saw the Christ as *central* to Creation, a metaphysical understanding of the Christian mysteries of Creation and Incarnation followed along lines that would have answered "no" to the question posed by some theologians: "If man had not sinned, would Christ have come?" Fortunately, even then and throughout Christian theology, there were those who, intuitively perhaps, responded with a resounding "yes" to the question. Christ is the linch-pin, the lodestone, the very reason for Creation. All is directed towards his coming and continuation until God shall be all in all. This Pauline and Johannine vision was the vision of Duns Scotus. It was the vision of Bonaventure, of Julian of Norwich, of Hildegarde of Bingen, of Meister Eckhart, of Gerard Manley Hopkins and of Teilhard de Chardin. Teilhard, however, concentrated on the Christ, not only as being the intention and purpose for Creation in its inception, but rather as the finalization and consummation in its fulfillment, going beyond the initial insight of Scotus. This view of Creation, as being ordered towards and taking place in Christ, has thus frequently been called an "incarnational" theology. While seemingly lost sight of during centuries when an Aristotelian world-view dominated religious thought, it came into its own again in the nineteenth and twentieth centuries. However, at present this incarnational model alone is insufficient. The reasons for this are many and complex. They represent the interface between science and religion which marked the nineteenth century, that burgeoning of human insight which was itself evidence of the very evolutionary theory which was then being uncovered. This evolutionary point of view, which contemporary persons can ignore only at their own risk, is expressive of humanity pressing forward, conscious of *itself* as an evolution. In the 19th century, Charles Darwin's theory of evolution transformed human perception concerning origins of the human, and the early analytical theories of Sigmund Freud helped to uncover the richness and complexity of the human person. During the same period Karl Marx revealed the deep significance of created matter with the attendant human responsibility for the earth itself, its resources and goals. It does not matter that these seminal theories have already been transcended, undergone revisions, and present themselves anew. At the time of their bursting onto the scene, they truly revolutionized human thinking, so that no one born in the twentieth century could possibly look at the world through glasses worn before the late nineteenth century.

One of the implications of accepting the fact of process is an understanding that creation is on-going, and that human persons must accept personal responsibility for creating a future which is "already but not yet." Furthermore, the responsibility *itself* is constantly increasing. First, a reflection on the reality of the process from Pierre Teilhard de Chardin:

> The world is a-building; this is the basic truth which must first be understood so thoroughly that it becomes an habitual, and, as it were, natural springboard for our thinking.... A process is at work in the universe ... the new earth is being formed and purified and is taking on definition and clarity.[1]

Secondly, the implications of such a process view as expressed by the contemporary theologian Thomas Berry:

> The world before us is the only world we have. We will love it, believe in it, advance it, make it beautiful. Else we will watch both ourselves and the world shrivel into subhuman forms. There is reason to believe that these things will be dealt with, that a new beauty will emerge, a new capacity for integrating man (sic) into the total life of the earth.[2]

These theologians remind us that this world has value. Secu-

[1] Teilhard de Chardin, "The Meaning and Constructive Value of Suffering." and Neville Braybrooke, ed., *Teilhard de Chardin: Pilgrim of the Future* (New York: Seabury Press, 1964), 23.

[2] Thomas Berry, "Christian Humanism," Riverdale Papers II (Riverdale, NY: Riverdale Center for Religious Research, 1979).

larity, in areas of ecology, technology, information, and education, merges with a new spirituality of creation into an eschatology, as the human cooperates in creating a new heaven and a new earth, the new earth that will herald the new heaven.

It can truly be said that God *needed* Jesus to be flesh in this world, on this earth and God *needs* us to be flesh in this world, on this earth. Incarnation, then, is the heart of Creation, a process of mutuality, which lends even greater dignity to our humanness. But the idea of an open universe demands the discarding of unworkable models, both of the universe and human nature as well. Creation has come to be seen as being continued in and through human endeavor. The human person is not just "part" of nature. The anthropology that accompanies such a world view, in addition to stressing an essential human mutuality with God, will also stress the essential mutuality of the sexes and essential human mutuality with the world. This stress on mutuality marks a positive shift in understanding of human relationship to God and the world.

Likewise, the relationship between science and theology has undergone radical changes from both sides. It is not just that theology has had to come to terms with the truth of Galileo, Copernicus, Darwin, and Einstein, modifying some of its own past "certainties," but scientists have also come to admit that some of their "certainties" are called into question by continuing developments in the universe. Technology, notes Langdon Gilkey, actually occasions the recurrence of basic religious questions. Mechanistic and materialistic explanations of an older scientific view are just as inefficient in the context of the rapidly unfolding research of astro-physics as the fundamentalist understanding of creationist theories which take biblical imagery literally. Advanced scientific theory can be seen as a supplement to deepened faith, and the religious point of view can inform the wonder of science. In the words of Robert Jastrow, American astronomer:

> The scientist has scaled the mountains of ignorance; he is about to conquer the highest peak—as he pulls himself over the final rock, he is greeted by a band of theologians who

have been sitting there for centuries.[3]

This open-ended, expanding universe is so clearly as yet unredeemed that the questions that address themselves to humanity point to the necessity of a more practical understanding of the Creation/Incarnation/Redemption mystery. The "mystery" must be seen, not as an isolated entrance of the divine into the human community, but as a continuing event to be entered into by all humanity in its struggle through suffering and death into new and fuller life.

> In our present age all purely incarnational cosmic theologies do not seem a live option. for we have moved from the closed world to an infinite universe. We now recognize more fully the tragic and radical evil in our midsts. We fear with reason for the fate of all humanity, indeed of the entire planet in the shadow of massive global suffering, and the threat of ecological crises and nuclear holocaust. It is not the case, of course, that Christians have ceased to believe in the incarnation of Jesus Christ. It is the case that Christians now recognize that the incarnation itself can be interpreted in the light of the ministry, cross, and resurrection of Jesus Christ.[4]

Teilhard de Chardin was surely not the only one who recognized the importance of transforming cosmology into a cosmic understanding of history and of enlarging the whole notion of Christology beyond the soteriological implications of redemption theories. However, the French paleontologist and theologian did provide the impetus for this new understanding of the significance of the relationship between the Christ and Creation, in an evolutionary world-view. The implications of this relationship will be seen with regard to sin

[3]Robert Jastrow, *God and the Astronomers* (New York: Warner Books, Inc., 1978), passim.

[4]David Tracy, *Cosmology and Theology* (New York: Seabury Press, 1983), conclusion.

and evil, and hope in an absolute future.[5]

Ongoing creation can be seen in all dimensions of human creativity, but is not concentrated there alone. The very earth itself is in process of change of such magnitude that it escapes us in our ordinary pursuits. Every day the newspaper, to say nothing of scientific journals, report some previously incredible new advance in human understanding of planet earth. The smallness of the planet which Marshall McLuhan dubbed "the global village" presses in on our consciousness. We tend now, hopefully, to think about belonging to the earth more than to any one nation. Indeed, the American astronauts who first viewed the planet earth from space, were first to say forthrightly that they felt themselves to be "citizens of the earth." It was an interesting choice of words, for Teilhard de Chardin had said in an early essay that it was essential for us to perceive ourselves as citizens of the earth. He also reminded his readers that the "age of nations" was past and we must strive together to build the earth or perish. Understanding that we are part of an open universe pushes us to new frontiers that have nothing to do with power or land "ownership." Rather, we become aware of the potential that is ours to shape a new world.

Within Roman Catholic Christian thought, this awareness is expressed clearly in Vatican II's pastoral Constitution,

[5]Teilhard has been an acknowledged major influence on many of the most prominent theologians of modern times, e.g., on the Continent, Piet Schoonenberg, Piet Smulders, Henri de Lubac, Bernard Häring, Ursula King, Ladislaus Boros, et al. Among Americans, Thomas Berry, Beatrice Bruteau, Donald Gray, Eulalio Baltazar and Christopher Mooney, all derive their theological approach directly from Teilhard, to say nothing of those countless millions of "ordinary people" who found a completely new and warm approach to the Christian mysteries on reading Teilhard. In her fascinating book *The Aquarian Conspiracy,* Marilyn Ferguson reports on a survey of a very diverse group of 185 men and women who consider themselves to be futurists and personalists: "When respondents were asked to name individuals whose ideas had influenced them, either through personal contact or through their writings, those *most often* named, *in order of frequency,* were Pierre Teilhard de Chardin, C. G. Jung, Abraham Maslow, Carl Rogers, Aldous Huxley, Robert Assagioli, and J. Krishnamurti." (The list continues to mention others less frequently named: Tillich, Hesse, Whitehead, Mead, Sri Aurobundo, Buckminister Fuller, Einstein and many more.) It is for these reasons that we will look more carefully at Teilhard's evolutionary theory for coherence in a Christian context. Cf. Marilyn Ferguson, *The Aquarian Conspiracy* (Los Angeles: J. F. Torcher, 1980), 420.

Gaudium et Spes. It notes that "the human race has passed from a rather static concept of reality to a more dynamic evolutionary one." Throughout the conciliar Constitution there is a tone of personalism and optimism about humanity, a dynamism that encourages people of all nations towards accepting the challenge of global cooperation in confronting humanity's problems and celebrating humanity's gift of creativity. The opening lines of *Gaudium et Spes* challenge us: "The joys and the hopes, the griefs and anxieties of the people of this age ... these too are the joys of the followers of Christ. Indeed, nothing genuinely human fails to raise an echo in their hearts ... this community realizes that it is truly and intimately linked with humanity and its history."[6] This book will explore that challenge in the context of our world as creation embodied. The new and very good news is that Jahweh is for us a God of promise, of compassion, that a Future awaits us, that we are loved, that we are believed in, and that we are *needed.* "The created universe waits, with eager expectation for the daughters and sons of God to be revealed." (Rom. 8:19)

---

[6]"Gaudium et Spes," Documents of Vatican II, ed. W. Abbott, S.J. (New York: Guild Press, 1961), 269.

God's Grandeur

The world is charged with the grandeur of God.
  It will flame out, like shining from shook foil;
  It gathers to a greatness, like the ooze of oil
Crushed. Why do men then now not reck his rod?
Generations have trod, have trod, have trod;
  And all is seared with trade; bleared, smeared with toil;
  And wears man's smudge and share man's smell: the soil
Is bare now, nor can foot feel, being shod.

And for all this, nature is never spent;
  There lives the dearest freshness deep down things;
And though the last lights off the black West went
  Oh, morning, at the brown brink eastward, springs
Because the Holy Ghost over the bent
  World broods with warm breast and with ah! bright wings.

Gerard Manley Hopkins

1

The Framework:
Letting Reality Be

"and God saw that it was good...." Genesis 1:10c

Traditional Understandings of Creation

The Word of Scripture that has been given to us as the normative point of departure for our theological reflection on Creation is rich with the richness of a fugue, a constantly recurring motif, full of beauty and power, a sacrament in the deepest sense that word can ever be sacrament. This Scriptural imagery is a fit medium of expression, directed toward women and men of all times, in all places, in the same way that all genuine poetry continues to speak over generations, but with the added dimension of a revelation directed toward the face and person of Jesus the Christ. It is our responsibility and privilege to uncover anew its meaning in this particular time and space.

Ecumenical development in theological and biblical studies has provided a new impetus to our understanding of how this scriptural language may be understood to cohere within the frame of an evolutionary world view. In an interesting convergence, astronomical studies tell the same developmental "story" recounted in the Bible.

We now know that the *universe* began some twenty billion years ago, so suddenly, so explosively that it was as if God simply spoke and all radiated from God. *Life* itself began in the sea about 3.5 billion years ago, as God said, "Let the waters teem with countless living creatures." (Gen. 1:20) Then, wonder of wonders, God "decided" to create humanity in God's own image, male and female, with binocular vision, grasping hands and enlarged brains. The development of modern humanity, as we understand humanity, stems from these higher primates, culminating in "true" humans only a few million years ago and "modern" humanity only 400,000 years ago. Although the writers of Genesis had no such scientific knowledge when they told their story, they did have a transforming experience of having been rescued, which prompted their own account, and led them to reflect on life's beginnings.

The creation stories in Genesis offer the reflections of a simple nomadic tribal people who have experienced almost inexpressible joy. They have been freed from slavery! They are their own masters! Out of this ecstatic experience, they see with certain clarity that it is the Lord God who has delivered them—the only God, the One God. With impeccable logic they conclude that the God of Israel who saved their lives must indeed be one and the same with the One who gave them life in the beginning. And in the beginning, this Lord created everything that they could see and taste and touch—and it was good. Liberation and creation are ineluctably linked.

The poetic and lyrical account of Genesis 1 acknowledges God as creating all that is, and the construct of Genesis 2 proclaims God's unconditional love for humanity in spite of the human inability to love consistently and faithfully. Both accounts, separated in composition by hundreds of years, proclaim the transcendence and immanence of Jahweh; and serve as primitive explanations for the wondrous mysteries of earth.

Genesis 1 is actually the later of the two accounts, and is identified by biblical scholars as the "priestly account." In both accounts, God's word is the cause of creation. There is no abstraction such as creation from nothing." Rather, God is more like a familiar, gentle potter who sets about creating beauty from clay which has been carefully prepared, just waiting for God's word to touch it into being.

IN THE BEGINNING God CREATED the heavens and the earth. The earth was without form and void, and darkness was upon the face of the deep; and the Spirit of God was moving over the face of the waters.

And God said, "Let there be light"; and there was light. And God saw that the light was good; and God separated the light from the darkness. God called the light Day, and the darkness he called Night. And there was evening and there was morning, one day.

And God said, "Let there be a firmament in the midst of the waters, and let it separate the waters from the waters." And God made the firmament and separated the waters which were under the firmament from the waters which were above the firmament. And it was so. And God called the firmament Heaven. And there was evening and there was morning, a second day.

And God said, "Let the waters under the heavens be gathered together into one place, and let the dry land appear." And it was so. God called the dry land Earth, and the waters that were gathered together he called Seas. and God saw that it was good. And God said, "Let the earth put forth vegetation, plants yielding seed, and fruit trees bearing fruit in which is their seed, each according to its kind, upon the earth." And it was so. The earth brought forth vegetation, plants yielding seed according to their own kinds, and trees bearing fruit in which is their seed, each according to its kind. *And God saw that it was good.* And there was evening and there was morning, a third day.

And God said, "Let there be lights in the firmament of the heavens to separate the day from the night; and let them be for signs and for seasons and for days and years, and let them be lights in the firmament of the heavens to give light upon the earth." And it was so. And God made the two great lights, the greater light to rule the day, and the lesser light to rule the night; he made the stars also. And God set them in the firmament of the heavens to give light upon the earth, to rule over the day and over the night, and to separate the light from the darkness. *And God saw that it was good.* And there was evening and there was morning, a fourth day.

And God said, "Let the waters bring forth swarms of living creatures, and let birds fly above the earth across the firmament of the heavens." So God created the great sea monsters and every living creature that moves, with which the waters swarm, according to their kinds, and every winged bird according to its kind. *And God saw that it was good.* And God blessed them, saying, "Be fruitful and multiply and fill the waters in the seas, and let birds multiply in the earth." And there was evening and there was morning a fifth day. And God said, "Let the earth bring forth living creatures according to their kind: cattle and creeping things and beasts of the earth according to their kinds." And it was so. And God made the beasts of the earth according to their kinds and the cattle according to their kinds, and everything that creeps upon the ground according to its kind. *And God saw that it was good.*

Then God said, "Let us make man in our image, after our likeness; and let them have dominion over the fish of the sea, and over the birds of the air, and over the cattle, and over all the earth, and over every creeping thing that creeps upon the earth." So God created man in his own image, in the image of God he created him; male and female he created them. And God blessed them, and God said to them, "Be fruitful and multiply, and fill the earth and subdue it; and have dominion over the fish of the sea and over the birds of the air and over every living thing that moves upon the earth." And God said, "Behold, I have given you every plant yielding seed which is upon the face of all the earth, and every tree with seed in its fruit; you shall have them for food. And to every beast of the earth, and to every bird of the air, and to everything that creeps on the earth, everything that has the breath of life, I have given every green plant for food." And it was so. *And God saw everything that he had made, and behold, it was very good.* And there was evening and there was morning, a sixth day.

Thus the heavens and the earth were finished, and all the host of them. And on the seventh day God finished his work which he had done, and he rested on the seventh day from all his work which he had done. So God blessed the seventh day and hallowed it, because on it God rested from all his work which he had done in creation.

These are the generations of the heavens and the earth when they were created. (Gen 1:1-2:4)

And now, the second account, called the "Yahwist account," focuses on Yahweh's works as they involve the Chosen People. This earlier account actually serves as prologue to the Exodus story, although it was written *after* the religious experience that led the people of Israel to consider themselves "the chosen" of the *one God* who had freed them. The style and message are different. The imagery is directed toward humanity and relationships:

> In the day that the Lord God made the earth and the heavens, when no plant of the field was yet in the earth and no herb of the field had yet sprung up—for the Lord God had not caused it to rain upon the earth, and there was no man to till the ground; but mist went up from the earth and watered the whole face of the ground—then the Lord God formed man of dust from the ground, and breathed into his nostrils the breath of life; and man became a living being. And the Lord God planted a garden in Eden, in the east; and there he put the man whom he had formed. And out of the ground the Lord God made to grow every tree that is pleasant to the sight and good for food, the tree of life also in the midst of the garden, and the tree of the knowledge of good and evil.
>
> A river flowed out of Eden to water the garden, and there it divided and became four rivers, The name of the first is Pishon; it is the one which flows around the whole land of Havi-lah, where there is gold; and the gold of that land is good; bdellium and onyx stone are there. The name of the second river is Gihon; it is the one which flows around the whole land of Cush. And the name of the third river is Tigris, which flows east of Assyria. And the fourth river is the Eu-phra'tes.

The Lord God took the man and put him in the garden of Eden to till it and keep it. And the Lord God commanded the man, saying "You may freely eat of every tree of the garden; but of the tree of the knowledge of good and evil you shall not eat, for in the day that you eat of it you shall die."

Then the Lord God said, "It is not good that the man should be alone; I will make him a helper fit for him." So out of the ground the Lord God formed every beast of the field and every bird of the air, and brought them to the man to see what he would call them; and whatever the man called every living creature, that was its name. The man gave names to all cattle, and to the birds of the air, and to every beast of the field; but for the man there was not found a helper fit for him. So the Lord God caused a deep sleep to fall upon the man, and while he slept took one of his ribs and closed up its place with flesh; and the rib which the Lord God had taken from the man he made into a woman and brought her to the man. Then the man said,

"This at last is bone of my bones and flesh of my flesh; she shall be called Woman, because she was taken out of Man."

Therefore a man leaves his father and his mother and cleaves to his wife, and they become one flesh. And the man and his wife were both naked, and were not ashamed. (Gen 2:5-25)

These skillfully woven stories must be seen and understood against the backdrop of the ancient Near East. The people of Israel, whether represented by the priestly writers of the later accounts in Genesis 1, or the earlier account in Genesis 2, were familiar with the creation myths of Babylon, Egypt and Canaan. In their own stories they counter the pagan myths by highlighting the eternal nature of Yahweh, and even more, God's loving attention to every detail of creation, especially the needs of Adam and Eva.

This beautiful narrative says over and over again that God looked at all of creation and found it good. The authors of Genesis are *very* sure on this point. Sun, moon, stars, fish, birds, animals and especially *hadamah* and *eva*, —the creature of the earth and the mother of the living—were good, so good that they were the living, breathing *images* of God.

But, as in any existential drama, the authors had to pay attention to some other realities around them. There was evil in the midst of God's creation. Pain, suffering, death. Some men took other men's flocks. Rulers were tyrannical. Enemies abounded. Some people took each other's spouses. Some brothers killed each other. Why? How to explain? How did they lose "paradise"? If God was good, why evil?

The primitive answer to these questions was to construct a mythical scene, in which the source of evil was a serpent tempting the first residents of Paradise. The serpent succeeded so well that Paradise was indeed lost, and life on earth filled with a puzzling mix of joy and agony, sun and storm, love and hate.

The story of a perfect garden, an Eden for man and woman, and of their subsequent fall from grace and God's favor was repeated by generation after generation. Although in Jewish religious thought the mythical account was never meant to be taken literally, the creative acts of God came to be seen as actually taking place within six days. The sin of Adam and Eve was variously described as a sin of pride, or perhaps a sexual sin. Gradually, the phenomenological myth about beginnings and purpose was transformed. The story became literalized. When Paul, the earliest New Testament author to write about the mystery of God in Christ, contrasted the "new Adam", Christ, with the old Adam, creation and redemption became separated, at least in the minds of many who read Paul.

Modern biblical scholars insist, however, that in the Jewish scripture, creation itself is a salvific act, and that creation and redemption are simultaneous and continuous processes. "The very existence of the world is salvific ... in Deutero-Isaiah, above all, creation and redemption appear almost as one and the same act of God's dramatic initiation."[1]

---

[1]Gerhard von Rad, *Theological Dictionary of the New Testament,* ed. G. Kittel (Grand Rapids: Eerdmans, 1964), I, 152, 165.

Importantly, when Paul wrote to the Christians at Rome, he drew a poignant image of personalized creation. He presented the whole of creation as groaning, unfinished, waiting with eager expectation (one translation says: "standing on tiptoe"), waiting for God's daughters and sons to be revealed, to lift creation from its ache and misery. Paul underscored the perennial problem of *universal* evil and intuitively, it seems, highlighted the human cooperation that is needed to alleviate it.

Paul's answer to the problem was not to be found in describing a period of "paradise", a time and place of total innocence. Most certainly, Paul did not intend to lay the whole of cosmic disruption at the feet of "Adam". Rather, his intent, as becomes even clearer in his later letters, was to link the human community directly with Christ in the task *of diminishing* the evil present in creation.

In his second letter to the Corinthians, he calls God's work "reconciliation". He tells them that God was *in Christ,* reconciling the world, and that the human community has been enlisted in that same work and service. (2 Cor 5:18-20)

Paul has already assured the churches at Rome and Ephesus that there was absolutely nothing that could separate humanity from God's love—nothing in death or life, nothing in the forces of the universe, nothing in all of creation (Rom 8:38-39)—and that God's hidden purpose was to bring everything in the universe, all in heaven and earth to a unity in Christ (Eph 1:3-10)

Despite the strength of these unequivocal statements, the problem of evil was not traditionally seen from such a positive anthropology. The question continued to be posed, "If God is good, why suffering, why death?"

Manichean and Gnostic Understanding

Manichean gnosticism posited a different answer completely to the problem of evil. This was the pessimistic notion of an equal, powerful source of evil opposing the goodness of creation. "Manicheism" was the direct lineal descendant of a vast reservoir of pre-Christian and early Christian thought known as Gnosticism. Rooted in paganism, with elements of Buddhist and Iranian writings, its elements are too unwieldly to be considered a Christian heresy as such, although many fathers of the Church, such as Irenaeus and Tertullian, were staunch foes of its misleading tenets as they affected Christian thinking. Most of the writings of the classical period of Gnosticism (2nd century) have not survived, but are reflected in the writings of Valentinus and Marcion. According to their presuppositions, God was not the creator of the world and had nothing to do with the world's continued existence. A basic premise of Gnostic view was a nebulous cosmic dualism between God and man, light and darkness, good and evil, so God could never have become authentically human. The Word merely *seemed* to become flesh (roots of the Docetist heresy).

Central to the philosophy of Manicheism, as in Gnosticism, was a thorough-going dualism, a separation of body and soul, matter and spirit, God and world. In some disciplines, it called for a strict asceticism; in others, as practiced by certain gnostics, a strict sexual abstinence. Misconceptions about the goodness of human sexuality were taught definitively. Matter was actually seen as evil. Spirit, or the soul, was the only "good." Sexual activity was tolerated for procreative purposes alone or rejected outright, since some Manicheans actually had a terror of sex. Priscillian (c. 385) founded such a Manichean sect in Spain, and taught that the devil is the creator of evil and of matter. The Council of Constantinople in 543 A.D. formally condemned the principal beliefs of the Manichees, but not before much harm had been done. (Cf. Appendix 3 for these condemnations.)

The effects of these eastern heresies tainted Christian thought even among "orthodox" teachers, despite the Church's continued insistence on the essential goodness, indeed, holiness of matter. The divine dimension of creation was overshadowed by a narrow sectarianism that infected religious thought and behavior. This negative anthropology had spread from the East to the West, and even the learned and brilliant Augustine of Hippo embraced its tenets for over nine years. The vestiges of that thought can be found in some of Augustine's writings, particularly in his own anthropology, which stems directly from the notion of a creation complete and originally perfect, then flawed. He read the biblical accounts literally, and intellectualized the story of the Fall into a theology of a *peccatum originale,* an original sin, lodged in the human soul. That construct has continued to haunt the human spirit for centuries, as if each human person, having been given the gift of life from the faithful One we call God, was simultaneously denied that love (or grace), almost genetically. Even though Augustine rejected Manicheism, all of this was somehow connected with his understanding of human sexuality, in which the body, the flesh, was a source of temptation, shot through with an inherited wound, a fatal weakness.

Of course, following his conversion, Augustine no longer believed with Gnostics or Manicheans. He wrote against Fortunatus, the renegade priest in 392, and long before he wrote against the Pelagians, he had come to his own conclusions regarding grace and freedom, sin and guilt. However, in his very effort to walk a fine line between the Manichean position that evil is an inevitable onslaught from a power outside the person, and Pelagius' idea that sin was somewhat accidental, Augustine nonetheless concluded that the transmission of sin took place in human propagation, from the initial fall, and so is inescapably connected with human sexuality.

In 418 A.D., he wrote a tract entitled "On the Grace of Christ and on Original Sin; Written Against Pelagius and Celestius." He responds strongly to the Pelagian objection that original sin is a disparagement of matrimony and praises the married state. But in the following chapter 40, he describes his literal understanding of the creation of the first man and woman, with the idea that *before* Adam's sin the procreative power was exercised by choice of the will, submissive to the power of the gentlest love, not by the ardour of lust. "The travail of the mother and the death of human offspring would never have supervened if sin had not preceded."

Interestingly, he concludes this discussion with this phrase: "...but of the sin the origin lies in the subtlety of the *devil* who deceives and in the *will* of the man who yields to the deception."[2]

It is not surprising then, to find Augustine's final decision for celibacy chronicled in a significant passage from his first soliloquy, in which he states unequivocally that "nothing is better designed for casting down a manly soul from its citadel than those feminine blandishments and bodily contact entailed in having a wife."[3] Therefore, Augustine decides "not to desire, not to seek, not to take a wife." Augustine's sentiment undermines any understanding of a dyadic creation, in which maleness and femaleness together proclaim the very nature of reality. The blessing of Genesis which promises fruitfulness heralds companionship and mutuality. Human life is grounded in respect and equality. So it is difficult to listen to the opposing Augustinian view. It is as though God could have reflected on all that had been created and found it good, except for human sexuality! If human sexuality, at the heart of the human, is somehow flawed, human nature itself is somehow perverted. Difficult as this may have been to hear, it seemed to be a prevailing theological view, accepted almost into modern times, because of the tremendous influence that was Augustine's. The difficulty is further compounded because the development of biblical studies was unknown to Augustine, who consistently used Scripture literally or allegorically. (The teachings of the Church which developed against this early, literalist and geocentric view are presented for reflection in Appendix 1.) As Karl Rahner points out, development of doctrine demands that the *substance* of previous tradition must constantly be reformulated in different language if it is to remain true to itself. As we shall see, it has taken many centuries and much theological labor and study to find new language which retains the truths contained in the primitive and picturesque language of Genesis: namely, the "creatureliness" of the human, the rejection of dualism, the equal dignity of both man and woman, and the understanding that all reality is God's, and good.

[2]Roger Balducelli, "Decision for Celibacy," *Theological Studies,* 36, 1975, 236.

[3]Augustine of Hippo, "The Anti-Pelagian Works On Original Sin Book II," 38-45.

Jansenism

Another major reason for the prolongation of the "human nature is basically evil" view of life can be ascribed to the late emergence of yet one more heretical anthropology. Cornelius Jansen of Louvain, Belgium, avidly studied Augustine's positions and wrote an admiring book entitled *Augustinus* which was published in 1640, two years after Jansen's death. His exaggerated distinctions between nature and grace followed along Augustinian lines, and left his adherents with an almost hopelessly pessimistic view of what it meant to be a human person with a sexual nature. Jansen's influence spread throughout France and all over Europe, affecting ordinary people and church leadership alike. Even the brilliant scientist Pascal fell prey to Jansenism. Controversy raged between the Jansenists and the Jesuits of western Europe, who tried desperately to stem the flow of these notions. Despite papal condemnations, the spirituality of the 1700's, 1800's, even the 1900's, was tainted with Jansenism. The heresy remained alive and well in the hearts of many earnest believers, infecting and reinforcing negative attitudes about human sexuality, particularly with regard to marriage and reproduction. Even in church documents the language concerning "primary" and "secondary" ends of marriage continued to be used, with the understanding that marriage was primarily ordered to procreation and the relationship was second in importance. Not until Vatican II (1962-1965) was this terminology excluded. (The condemnations against the Pelagians, Manicheans and Jansenists are listed in Appendix 3.)

Twentieth-Century Advances

Although destructive repercussions on Christian living continued to be felt into the twentieth century, a changing, developing theology that preceded the Second Vatican Council began to raise serious questions. This shift reflected the theological "coming of age" of a church too long "stuck" in a medieval and false cosmology, with a spirituality rooted in a misshapen anthropology.

Pierre Teilhard de Chardin, having understood the full implications of an evolutionary world-view on such an anthropology, boldly wrestled with the questions, in his essays on original sin, throughout the 1920's, 30's and 40's. It was precisely these forthright reflections that occasioned the sanctions forbidding him to publish (1922). Nonetheless, his more realistic concept of the "sin of the world" gradually overtook the concept of an inherently damaged humanity, born "naturally" incapable of good. Together with this lucid description of an *entire creation* still struggling to overcome the multiplicity and fragmentation in a yet unfinished universe, came the work of Henri de Lubac, S.J., with an equally clear presentation, insisting that the "natural and supernatural" do not run on two separate tracks, but rather co-mingle and inform each other. De Lubac, a theologian who used an historical methodology to support his positions, was also considered suspect in the mid-twentieth century. The positive, hope-filled anthropologies of these two scholars, along with others, mainly from France and Belgium, were dismissed in some circles as (pejoratively) "la nouvelle théologie" because they called for a reformulation of doctrine. Nor did they meet with official acceptance or affirmation. Indeed, within the Roman Christian community, strong language was used to suggest that it was not at all clear how these new and startling formulations about the universe and human/divine cooperation in creating a new heaven and new earth could be reconciled with Scripture.[4] Fortunately, the obstacles to an acceptance of this new understanding—lack of expertise in scientific methodology and a reluctance to employ a new method of scriptural criticism—were practically overcome within the first half of the twentieth century. Liturgical renewal at the monastic level found its way to the reforms of Vatican II, and the confluence or convergence of these scholarly works in the areas of Scripture, systematic theology and liturgical ritual, found voice most especially in the docu-

[4]*Humani Generis,* 1950, Pius XII (NCWC translation).

ment *Gaudium et Spes,* as previously noted.[5]

This new understanding would not be one which fell prey to a simplistic optimism about the human spirit when attempting to displace the former negative anthropology. Rather, it would be one which took seriously human alienation as part of the ongoing process of human growth and development. Theologians like Karl Rahner and Piet Schoonenberg brought to the discussion at Vatican Council II a theology of grace that took the existential experience of the human person as its starting point, together with the idea of the universe itself as being a developmental process.

The stage was now set for new models of interpreting creation, and a more human expression of both thanksgiving and human challenge in the Christian community. As Christians observed the challenge being met by many who declined "faith," or who chose to speak of humanist goals, they were led to further questions about the special significance of Christ in such a rapidly expanding, needy world. Karl Rahner named these workers of the earth "anonymous Christians," and Teilhard called for a "new Nicaea," with an understanding of Jesus' humanity as initiating a completely new "moment" in human evolution. The resurrection and lordship of the Christ had to have "cosmic significance." Far from lessening the older formulations about God in Christ, the vision of a cosmic Christ/Omega still in process of personalization fits the contemporary situation perfectly. It hearkened back to the Pauline and Johannine themes in which the Christ is all-in-all, the very raison d'être for creation, with *all* humanity likewise designed in that very paradigm.

In this Christological perspective, Christ enjoys, as it were, a third, cosmic nature, in which all of humanity is somehow influenced by his universal risen presence, whether consciously alluded to and celebrated or not. Even this formulation may still sound to some as condescending towards, or ignorant of, other world religions. But it is consistent with an evolution grown conscious of itself and the need to take the Christic

---

[5]"Gaudium et Spes," *Documents of Vatican II,* ed. W. Abbott, S.J., 262, par. 202.

Message of non-exclusive love seriously, and to recognize it as the necessary healing and propelling force that alone can save an earth on the brink of disaster. It demands the fullest immersion possible of the Christian stream into the human stream.

The fullness of humanity awaits us and will ultimately be seen in that "vanguard" of people living the *way of life* initiated by the One who looked at creation's pain and went about healing, restoring sight, giving new ears, opening hearts closed by old enmities. The idea of *loving* as being definitive of humanity self-conscious of itself is a late, recent evolutionary leap forward. That it is the sinē quā non for a human future is clear. A straightforward look at the stages or phases of evolution that the earth and humanity have already been through will perhaps help us to see this with even greater clarity.

Teilhard De Chardin's Evolutionary Model

> Of all things the most difficult to contain is the expansion of an idea.... It is enough for truth to appear just once, to a single mind. From that moment nothing can prevent its spreading until it lights up the world.... For whatever is truer will come to light; and whatever is better will ultimately come into being."
>
> Teilhard de Chardin

Pierre Teilhard de Chardin, priest and scientist, wanted to develop a unified world view which would be able to integrate the scriptural insight and meaning into what we actually know about a scientific, technological world in process. He wanted to show that the Creation story of Genesis was not irreconcilable with an understanding of evolution, but rather that the two were just different ways of looking at one truth, each designed to complete the other. He chose to proceed phenomenologically, in a coherent synthesis of two sources: scripture and science.

Observation of the phenomenon of the universe in a com-
prehensive gaze which includes humanity as a phenomenon
leads to an inductive law of "complexity-consciousness." That
is, there is a correlation between increasing organic complexity
and an increase in consciousness. The more complex, highly
concentrated units appear last in order of evolution, and
through a backward extrapolation, provide the basis for obser-
ving that everything that is has a within and a without, and
that the direction of the process is towards greater consciousness, as well as greater complexity. Co-extensive with the
"withoutness" of the stuff of the universe, there is a
"withinness."

A future extrapolation would suggest that we have entered
a new phase of evolution, that the hope for a new humanity is
opening before us. The increased complexity of human technology provides the possibility of an increase in human consciousness in the most profound way. The awareness of the
solidarity of the human community accelerates all around us.

A brief outline of this general scientific theory in which a
cosmic love is at work is here presented. Fundamental to the
hypothesis is the belief that, beyond the simple fact of evolution
itself, the current running through increasingly complex organisms, with an accompanying increase in consciousness, is going
somewhere. The evolutionary process is convergent, that is, it
has a line of direction, critical points, a precise orientation and
privileged axis. The geosphere, the developing earth, unfolds
into the biosphere, the living matter developing on earth. When
the biosphere reaches a critical point, thought, reflective life, is
born. This leap forward, this phase of the process of becoming,
is distinguished by the neologism "noogenesis," the development of the human. And with the onset of noogenesis, the
process changes radically. Put simply, *thought* changes things:

> Until the coming of the human, the pattern of the Tree of
> Life was always like that of a fan, a spread of morphological
> radiations diverging more and more, each radiation cul-
> minating in a new "knot" and breaking into a fan of its
> own. but at the human level a *radical change,* seemingly

due to the spiritual phenomenon of Reflection, overtook this law of development. It is generally accepted that what distinguishes man psychologically from other living creatures is the power acquired by his consciousness of turning upon itself ... only man ... knows what he knows.[6]

Because now the human *is* evolution, human persons can be seen as the spearhead of the whole evolutionary process, the crest of the wave. This is no accident. Precisely because humanity is oriented to a future point of maximum progress, there must be a personal center. Without such personal pull, evolution would cease. This is, in fact, at the root of human anxiety. Not only must people hope in the future, but here and now, they must be able to achieve union with each other in a common thrust, a pull forward. Thus are linked a cosmic energy which is Love, with the need for Hope in an Absolute Future which is both personal and personalizing.

The importance of Love in this synthesis is truly radical. Love is the driving force towards personalization. But to love is to be drawn together, center-to-center. This is not easy to achieve. How, in the noosphere, does love begin to take over?

The suggested answer comes in a meditative reflection:

> Reflecting, even briefly, on the state of affairs which might evoke this universal love in the human heart, a love so often vainly dreamed of, but which now leaves the fields of Utopia to reveal itself as both possible and necessary, we are brought to the following conclusion: That for humans upon earth, all the earth, to learn to love one another, it is not enough that they should know themselves to be members of one and the same thing: in planetizing themselves they must acquire consciousness, without losing themselves, or becoming one and the same *person*. For (and this is writ large in the Gospel) there is no total love that does not proceed from, and exist within, that supreme pole of consciousness,

[6]Teilhard de Chardin, "The Formation of the Noosphere," *Future of Man* (New York: Harper and Row, 1947), 164.

upon which all the separate consciousnesses of the world
may converge and within which they may love one another:
the rise of a God.[7]

The link between a divine evolution creative of the human is
a humanity preparing for a Jesus who will be so fully human
that he will be *the breakthrough,* the next "critical point", a
loving human person, the Paradigm for what it is to be human,
and, at the same time, a revelation of the mystery of God. He
is "Le Christ evoluteur", not just a thinker, but a lover, and
therefore "the Evolver". Noogenesis moves into Christogenesis,
meant to be coincident with cosmogenesis. This dynamic
process has introduced into the world that way of universal
love which otherwise might have been inconceivable. The
building up of the body of Christ, Christogenesis, requires the
becoming of Spirit/person, noogenesis, as its matrix.

Basic to this view is the concept of Creation as a unification
process, ever and always operative, with the entrance of Christ
seen to be the dynamic force of the unitive, creative act of
evolution, as well as the dynamic locus where redemption
takes place. The very structure of the words, Creation, Incarnation, Redemption indicates process, unfinished business.

It is necessary to stop here in order to perceive the significance of this view of Christianity, evolution and history.
Several key concepts emerge immediately. If every organism is
an entity with a complexity and consciousness that are never
separate phenomenologically, neither then are the dimensions
of Jesus to be conceived of in any dichotomous manner. If all
matter and spirit are perceived as unities throughout evolution,
the matter and spirit who is Jesus cannot be seen separately. It
is exactly here that this evolutionary model or paradigm has
the most say to the contemporary theologians who are stressing
the full humanity of Jesus. Although many critics of Teilhard
have seen only his emphasis on the cosmic Christ, and concluded to a description of his Christology as "descending,"

---

[7]Teilhard de Chardin, "Life and the Planets," *Future of Man* (New York: Harper
and Row, 1947), 124-125.

theologians like Ansfred Hulsbosch and Piet Schoonenberg have seen the impact of this concept of Christ as being the center of the whole process of cosmogenesis.[8] It is the *humanity* of Jesus which has been raised. In this Christological perspective, cosmogenesis has Christogenesis as its goal. Creation is *for* Incarnation. The mysteries of Creation, Incarnation, Redemption are inextricably linked. They develop on the sphere which is earth.

But, very importantly, this "redemption" cannot be restricted to planet earth. It is the *whole* of creation which is groaning, yearning for completion. A geo-centric world view is no longer a possible back-drop for the image of Christ risen and permeating all of reality. (While we will continue to examine here the meaning of Christ for humanity and earth, we will return to this concept of Christ as being critical to universal creation in a later section.) At this point however, we must raise the question about redemption of the *whole* universe, the building of the earth, and return to the role that the doctrine of original sin has played in our understanding of Christ's role and our own.

The "Fall": Impact of the Doctrine of Original Sin

Here the scientific theory opens itself up to the data of revelation. Jesus, the Christ entered into humanity when the time was ripe, not simply in the capacity of one more human element associated with it, but with the dignity and function of directive principle, or center upon which every form of love and every affinity converge. But the Christ has not reached the peak of growth, and the force behind all created activity is directed to engendering this growth. The building of the Body is directly connected to building the earth. The Christ needs the growing love of humanity in order to assume his own cosmic role to continue the work of Creation and Redemption.

[8]Robert North, *In Search of the Human Jesus* (Washington, DC: Corpus, 1970), 6,14.

This creative/redemptive process is, of its nature, healing, salvific, humanizing, personalizing. That humanity has had a long-lived reluctance to accept fully the positive implications of this mystery can be partly explained by the way in which the biblical doctrine on original sin has traditionally been presented, with its resultant negative impression of the "merely" human.

> Without exaggeration we can say that the doctrine on original sin as it is still formulated today is one of the principal obstacles right now for the intensive and progressive progress of Christian thought. . . . The story of the Fall paralyzes the necessary establishment of a world view that is fully human and humanizing.[9]

However, by placing original sin within an evolutionary framework, where it can be seen as the evil that is concomitant with a converging evolving universe, we get a quite different anthropology. *Creatio ex nihilo* becomes *creatio continua,* a continuous synthesizing and organization of the infinite multiplicity which corresponds to the biblical chaos. Both physical and moral evil—of which "original sin" is an element—are inevitably built into a world in progress. The concept of the "sin of the world" has been introduced by biblical scholars to show that we are all born into and share in the sinful human situation which marks the slow progress of humanity through history.

We have already noted that it is not only humanity that suffers from multiplicity and fragmentation. The whole of creation proceeds with a "shadow side," from the earliest stages of the becoming of reality through every phase of developmental life. Along with growth and positive development, there are multiple manifestations of physical evil which *precede* any human life on the planet, and which continue even up to this

[9]Teilhard de Chardin, "Reflections on Original Sin," *Christianity and Evolution* (New York: Harper and Row, 1971), 188.

day. This knowledge, of course, necessitates the rethinking of evil as being the result of the sin of our "first parents," and looks more to the sense of the "sin of the world," the unfinished environment into which everything and everyone that is born enters.

Human need for reconciliation, and the world's need for redemption are all too obvious. We are not finished. God is still ahead of us, in the future. Here there is then a theology of sin and redemption, of creation and soteriology which is radically different from past formulations, but true to the truth of revelation and tradition.

This way of looking at the evil around us takes into consideration that if indeed evolution is the way by which God creates, then a world still moving towards God is by definition a world still partially disorganized, imperfect. The perfections of God cannot run counter to the nature of a world in the process of growth. There will have to be diminishments, loss and shock until the world is freed, until creation is consummated. This is not to say that we should not struggle against evil wherever it evidences itself. Humanity itself is diminished by suffering which is absurd and stupid, but when it has been resisted to a final point of resignation, even that loss can be creative and productive.

In this light, the cross is seen as paradigm for the hard work of evolution even more than expiation. It becomes the model for the actual struggle that is the human drama, the price of development, both spiritual and physical. A way of imagining this is to see the vertical upright bar of the Cross as a symbol of the upward thrust of evolution, cosmic and personal. Each time the horizontal bar *crosses* the vertical, it represents an obstacle, a hurdle, that must be overcome, a moment of death and resurrection. Humanity dies in many ways, psychologically and spiritually, long before physical death overtakes an individual. It is through these little "deaths" and "risings" that persons become integrated, self-actualized.

An added significance of this approach lies in its stress on the unity of matter and spirit, the breakdown of dualism, and the gradual movement towards ever greater unity.

Paradigmatic Humanity of Jesus

Pursuing this line of thought to its logical conclusion yields a Christology that sees the divinity of Jesus residing precisely in the fullness of his integrated humanity, which has been raised to continue the creative process. The process of creation which is initiated by God, "Alpha," moves arduously through pain and suffering to the moment of union when God shall be all in all, in Christ "Omega."

The paradigmatic role of Jesus is dependent upon this basic conception of the risen Christ as embracing the whole universe and human environment as represented by the cosmos, as well as God and humanity, represented by Christ. Cosmogenesis and Christogenesis become one. That is to say that the building up of the cosmos is coincident with the building up of the Body of Christ. "The Christ", a title we have been using, is extended far beyond its most obvious connection of continuity with the historical Jesus to a discontinuous, radically transformed, spiritual presence filling the cosmos.

Much that is new and exciting is taking place within the scientific community and touches the present discussion. The perception of the Christ as being a breakthrough, a critical threshold, the Evolver of the Cosmos, the Guarantor of future growth fits well with the explorations of physicists with regard to a re-thinking of the Second Law of Thermodynamics, and the future of the universe.[10]

Likewise, the work of molecular biologists has led to the discovery that in addition to molecular DNA there is a startling and unexpected find of mitochondria, a new kind of DNA which comes directly from the mother exclusively, thus linking the entire human community genetically. This shared genetic legacy comes in all probability from many "first mothers," but

---

[10]Marilyn Noz, "Prigogine, Teilhard, and the Second Law of Thermodynamics," *Teilhard Newsletter,* Dec. 1979, 4-5. Marilyn Noz, professor of radiology at New York University Medical School, responds to the New York Times article, "Scientists See a Loophole in the Fatal Law of Physics," May 29, 1979. The implications of a "force" pushing life *forward* are exciting and optimistic.

links us together as a "body." The study of recombinant DNA was surely one of the great scientific discoveries of our time, but this new refinement pushes the question of human origins and connectedness even further. Something is happening in the human community's self-awareness that demands more spiritual connectedness, greater loving, a new way of thinking, since we do belong to each other in our very inception. As in all biological processes, when complex energies follow their tendency to group around a center, they break through their original unity and form a new state of consciousness. In this case, the energy is the Spirit released, given by Jesus, and the new process, Christogenesis. Through the Resurrection, a new zone of thought, or "field of attraction," began to spread, and is continuing to spread over the earth, capable of influencing persons to deeds of generosity, renunciation, love for other people, and love of the earth itself. This spirit is not identical with the body/person of Jesus, and the process is by no means restricted to persons in the Christian Church (although of a certainty, the Christian Church is meant to provide a dynamic locus for conscious human participation in the building up of the *earth* which is the Body of Christ). But the Spirit breathes where it will, sometimes surprising us with its vital presence in unlikely places.

We are at a critical point in human evolution. A "Christic" life of creativity demands a new kind of spirituality which addresses itself to real issues. What happens in the world is the stuff of prayer—the disenchantment of the young and brilliant; the deeper entrenchment of the worried and frightened; the corporate brutality of war; the personal brutalities invading family life; the impersonalism of an age of mechanization and technology; the systematic inequities that cause hunger, not only in underdeveloped countries, but in the most advanced industrialized country in the world, the United States of America. All of this demands compassionate action—for the world, in the world. Chapter 2 will begin to look at the questions facing women and men at this time as being at the heart of the drama of the universe, and in particular at the very relationships between men and women as being crucial to that exciting, terrifying, mysterious drama.

2

The Question:
The Drama of the Universe

"And God created humanity in God's own image,
male and female God created them." Genesis 1:27

The Human Dyad—Co-Creators

We have already noted that one of the most important
areas that awaits a new creation theology is a deepened understanding of the basic male/femaleness of the human dimension
of creation. The significant contribution that the concept of
complexity/consciousness, with its accompanying corollary of
differentiating union can bring to the discussion is that it avoids
the extremes of disparagement of sex (and specifically woman)
and the over-romanticization and idealization of sex (and
specifically woman). Simply stated, in an evolving world in
which all organisms proceed from lesser to greater complexity,
and correspondingly, from lesser to greater consciousness,
another phenomenon accompanies the process. The more
united or integrated an organism, the more differentiated it
becomes. In a correlative manner, the more differentiated an
organism, the greater its capacity and suitability for union. In
the case of the human organism, this can be preeminently
seen, both internally, in the highly differentiated organs and
systems which comprise the body, dominated by the guiding
force of the unitive brain, and á fortiori in the clear differentiation that exists between male and female, both physiolo-
gically and psychologically. These differences demand union,

convergence, mutuality. The biblical presentation in Genesis is precisely ordered to this realistic understanding, as we have seen. This understanding of creation of human sexual persons is *relational*. Personal responsibility for creating a future can only be realized in productive union, in communities of hope and love. Let us begin with the *symbolic* scriptural envisionment of the most basic human "community":

> Out of the intimacy of man's own flesh, a woman is summoned, life-sized and fully alive. She is meant to be the other self in relation to whom the *mutuality* of *intimacy* is to be possible and indeed inevitable. Translated into contemporary language, the paradigmatic recital announces that it takes one man and one woman and their intimacy to constitute one whole human being. The two belong to each other's adulthood.[1]

The beautiful language of imagery and reality is that of Roger Balducelli, biblical theologian. It is confirmatory of the scientific and phenomenological language that tells us that union differentiates, at all levels. It reveals the same insight that Phyllis Trible, another contemporary biblical theologian, gleans from a careful exegesis of the text involved, namely that "Unity embraces sexual differentiation; it does not impose sexual identicalness." In other words, unity is dependent on diversity, differentiation. The whole of Phyllis Trible's brilliant analysis is extraordinarily important for reflection, not only on metaphorical God-talk, but especially for the theological purposes of understanding the role and image of woman up to the present.[2] The incomprehensible Reality that we have named God most certainly transcends human sexuality, and yet embraces all of masculine and feminine reality. There is no scriptural basis for seeing woman as inferior because she is different, no basis for claiming "maleness" for God as over against

[1] Roger Balducelli, "Decision," 223.

[2] Phyllis Trible, *God and the Rhetoric of Sexuality* (Philadelphia, PA: Fortress Press, 1978), passim.

"femaleness" (or vice-versa). It is critical that we re-structure God-talk to omit the sexual overtones of masculinity, and just as critical that we understand the true nature of the scriptural language which underscores the mutuality of the male and female (albeit in imagery that departs from the reality of human emergence from the female womb)!

Another biblical scholar, Elisabeth Fiorenza, provides further assistance on an issue alluded to earlier, namely, the necessity of understanding the literary genre which is the medium of Scripture. She argues for a pastoral, theological interpretation of scriptural imagery.[3] It is not possible to do justice to all the nuances and differences even among feminist scholars, but, at the very least, it may be presumed that their engagement with the text in an effort to uncover the roots of patriarchal suppression and repression of woman is not meant to end there. Wherever there is heard any tone of imposing woman's experience as over against man's, there must be criticism of dependence on such exclusive "female experience," which would be just as faulty as interpreting reality from exclusive male experience. However, it is not to these necessary scholarly efforts that our next reflection is directed, but rather towards some popularization of women's studies which fall far short of the mark in a non-creative, unimaginative style. One of the difficulties with much of what passes for "feminist" writing at this point in the struggle is that it ignores or serves to undermine the very ideas of *intimacy, mutuality,* and *partnership.* This posture makes the fatal mistake of falling itself, full scale, into an "-ism" mentality, that is to say, creating a closed circuit, an ideology which would deny inter-dependency between the sexes. Instead of moving beyond the themes of oppressive historical, societal, and religious denigration, which most certainly have to be exposed, it lingers there, seemingly forgetting that the goal is mutuality and new-found intimacy, not hostility.

One of the realities of this universe in which we live, and the

---

[3]Elisabeth Schüssler Fiorenza, *In Memory of Her* (New York: Crossroads, 1983), passim.

ultimate question at the root of human liberation, is this very question of human mutuality. It is most interesting that at this critical time in which we find ourselves faced with questions that are truly cosmic, global questions about population control, universal questions about polluting the environment in which we live, international questions about the structures of education, about how values are conveyed, about national priorities and what can be understood to be integrity and wisdom with regard to war, peace, poverty and race—the whole spectrum of issues bursting around us until they all but overwhelm us—it is then at *this* particular time, that the place, the impact, and the input of the female half of the population is being born anew.

When this phenomenon is observed within an evolutionary context, it becomes clear that it is no "coincidence." In a theological/anthropological perspective: God is still creating the universe anew, advancing it, not just sustaining it. Women and men are called to be co-creators, together. At this particular time, women are being called to help carve out the future in a new and creative way. If women refuse to take that challenge seriously, or men refuse to accept women's contributions, then all threatening possibilities may become more than threats or possibilities.

There has been acknowledgement, however grudging, in some areas, that the equality of the sexes is a fact. There are laws which enable women to receive equitable treatment. There has been recognition that women have a role to play in society equal to that played by men. The reason that this must be so is very simple, and yet what is most real is not always most apparent. The reason is that the human race is a dyad, not a monad. It is, as we have seen, made of differentiated male and female components. Shunting off the contributions of half of that humanity has created a major lack. Were the question to be posed, "Does our society lack a certain warmth, certain dimension of human relating in its approaches to problems?" The answer must be "Yes," precisely because the female component and input has been lacking in government, in educational institutions, in business and industry, in religion, in medicine, in law.

Mere laws, although *essential,* are insufficient to change deep-seated prejudice, long-lived discrimination, and downright oppression. We do need an Equal Rights Amendment in the United States, and more than that, by way of law, in third world countries, and impoverished areas throughout the world. But the point is, neither the legislations nor the attitudinal changes should be based on a concept that men and women are the "same". Women deserve and need equality because they share a common humanity, lived out in a highly differentiated mode of personal being.

This represents a wholly different position from one that declares: "Men and women are equal because men and women are the *same.*" The difficulty with that position is that it is based on philosophical and physiological flaws. Further, it has no source in any authentic religious understanding of humanity. The valid philosophical assumption for admitting that our society lacks a great deal because the female component has not been present begins with an understanding that men and women are equal, precisely because they are *different.* One immediate objection has been that differences are all culturally induced; they are not real differences; men and women are exactly the same. To make such a statement begs the question and denies creation. If women and men were exactly the same, then there would not really have been any "lack." If women and men are exactly the same, then men *can* "do it all" by themselves, because women can only offer more of the same, in a quantitative manner. It does not appear that at this point in history more of the same is what is needed, although some proponents of women's liberation seem to have adopted the male mode of behavior unquestioningly in their efforts to be "equal." It is necessary to begin with a deep understanding that woman is unique and different from her male counterpart, without arguing whether these differences are culturally induced, (which many of them are) or whether they are inherent, (which most of them are).

The fact that there are differences is then a given, simply because we have been created so and exist along an evolutionary, time-space continuum. This is the structure of reality. (Speaking of the dyadic structure of reality is not meant to obviate or ignore the phenomenon of persons oriented towards same-sex relationships. It is rather to highlight the phenomenological reality of the majority of persons acknowledging sexual differentiation as a necessary basis of union, psychologically as well as physically, rather than as reason for discrimination.) Clearly there are those persons whose own self-identity does not fall within this structure. That does not mean that they are not called to be with persons of the same and the opposite sex in personal and professional areas in which mutuality is essential. This concept of mutuality is significant for the discussion of human sexuality in all areas. Certainly any genuine human relationships between homosexual persons, will include this concept of mutual respect, of not "becoming the other," of not being limited to sexual expression. Too little attention has been given this reality with resultant suffering and discrimination against homosexual partners. Such lack of compassion does nothing for anybody. This particular study cannot address itself to this question in depth, and is here concerned with the existing problem between men and women with regard to understanding differences.

There is a mix of cultural and genetic differences. The physiological differences, which are so clearly observable, must have more meaning than the simply morphological. If the notion of a body-person as an entity is taken seriously, there must be psychic differences which accompany the physiological. Granted these differences, the question is: how are they best utilized to further *human* liberation, *personal* liberation? Men who are really interested in women's freedom are the first to acknowledge that a true liberation of women will accomplish a needed liberation of men, a freedom from stereotypical role that have inhibited their own personal development.

Liberation: A Biblical Concept

This is not far afield, by any means, from a theological concept. Liberation is a basic biblical concept. It is a motif, a construct, a structure that runs through the scriptures, because what is being talked about is really another word for "salvation." What are persons being saved from or saved for? What are they being freed from and freed for? All of this is basic to the understanding of what it means to be a human. How do people understand and live their maleness or femaleness? The answer given must not be solely in terms of a personal liberation which bestows freedom, but of a freedom that carries with it responsibility. The freedom that contemporary persons must seek is the freedom that will enable them to become further differentiated, because the further differentiated one becomes, the more *person* one becomes, and the more one is available to the world.

It does not help, as some anthropological studies of women's roles have done, simply to look at our ancestors along an evolutionary scale and note the distinct roles of primitive ancestors. That is not helpful once an evolutionary, personalistic framework has been entered because the first thing we have to acknowledge about being human is that once the phenomenon of *thought* is present, then everything else is changed. Thought changes things! Women's intellectual abilities to *think* through the problems that occur as life progresses have not been sufficiently challenged, and certainly not honestly acknowledged. Consequently, human liberation has been limping along, without all the power available being utilized.

In a reflective essay entitled *The Evolution of Chastity,* stunning in its prior understanding of the contemporary issues facing men and women today, Teilhard de Chardin highlights the evolutionary dimension of our new-consciousness.[4] We have been forced, by experience, to realize the inexhaustible richness of matter in its psychological energies, and we realize that everything lies ahead of us, waiting to be found. This transformation of past negative attitudes about matter leads to a new and wonderful intuition, shared by many, rejected still

[4]Teilhard de Chardin, "The Evolution of Chastity," *Towards the Future* (New York: Harcourt, Brace, Jovanovich, 1975), 70-77.

by too many: "At the term of spiritual power of matter lies the spiritual power of the flesh and of the feminine. . . . Woman is, for man, the symbol and personification of all the fulfillments we look for from the universe. . . . Woman brings fullness of being, sensibility and self-revelation to the man who has loved her."[5] The author of those words is not being over-idealistic. He is making an extraordinary point, as the entire context of the essay demonstrates. Whereas in the past woman has seemed to exist only for the propagation of the race, such a false simplification falls apart in the face of acknowledged experience. Woman's "maternity" is almost nothing in comparison to her spiritual "fertility." The degree of psychological consciousness that the world has reached demands a developing of *spiritual* energy more than it does physical reproduction of the species. New kinds of unions, friendships, richer, more diverse, ordered *beyond* the paired couples must and will emerge.

The particular organic life which we call human on this planet, in which all of us who are thinkers are involved, is a process of personal and corporate humanization, that can only be accomplished in union. So for woman to assume her full place, her full dignity (no question but that this full dignity has not been attained), the answer does not lie in separateness. Although there is a period of time in all liberation movements where there is some kind of standing apart, this should be known to be only temporary. There is a standing apart for purposes of achieving objectivity, for purposes of clarification, but only with the understanding that ultimately that kind of differentiation will lead to convergence, and that convergence is not meant to be an obliteration, or fusion, but a mutuality that enhances all.

Differentiating Union: Basis of Community

The differentiation of woman in order that she be more

[5] Ibid., 70.

fully personalized and given scope to exercise all her talents is a principle that is present in all of life. Only in union do we become differentiated.... Only in community, only in a situation where we are personally involved in something which is *relational, reciprocal* and *mutual.* Examples of this can be seen on varying levels of human growth. One that is obvious is the example of a team. For a team to be effective, to be operative, to succeed in what it tries to do, there has to be unity; but the unity is marked precisely by differentiation. That is what makes a team, and not amalgam. There have to be persons with highly specialized skills which they bring together for a single purpose. The better an individual player, the better the team. In a circular fashion, the better, the stronger, the more united the team, the more possibility there is for a highly skilled and differentiated person to emerge. At that level of human relationship affectivity is not essential. In other words, men and women engaged in a sport, or a research team don't have to like each other. (It would help if they did, but it is not essential). In the realm of friendship, and of love relationships, the same principle is at work, but now much more important because it involves the whole person. Any relationship should have for its result not sameness, but precisely the distinctiveness, the uniqueness that is the mark of a fully mature person. To work and to live in situations in which growth is interconnected and interdependent, in the very best sense of dependency, upon the personal growth of other persons, is of the essence of development. No one can become person alone. The woman cannot become the person she desires to be or feels called to be in isolation. The obviousness that union is better than isolation is something that need not be stressed. The practical working out of that means that each person becomes more himself or herself, rather than some kind of "amorphous whole" in which one person becomes a shadow of another, or is completely absorbed into the other's life. The goal is not to become the other, but to become more personalized. This remains a very real problem in contemporary society and is part of the cry of women from all over the world. Many see themselves as somehow in the background of some man's life, be it a husband, an employer, church authority, or political governance.

A look at some of the strong women figures in classical or biblical literature presented as being "ideal," indicates the contrary. Sarah, Ruth, Esther, Mary, Beatrice, Laura, Teresa, Catherine, are not subordinate and not accessories. They are necessary to a mutuality, and the mutuality exists because there is a common will towards convergence.

Women and men have every reason and right to establish relationships which are fulfilling for themselves and for the other persons to whom they relate, whether this be a spouse, children, friends, or parents: whether the relationship is between persons of the same sex, between persons of different ages, between professional companions, or other relationships outside the immediate familial one. All should be accompanied by responsibility and accountability, but also by mutuality, something reciprocal, something that is freeing for all persons. Only then can relationships be properly called human. The question of responsibility for the future is a real question for both women and men because it so presses upon us right now. The possibility of categorical or ideological answers being used as the answer for some of our more urgent human problems is present with us. Physicians, lawyers, demographers and theologians constantly probe for answers to questions concerning the direction of our future. Knowing as we do that the future is impinging upon our present now, that the pace of evolution and the pace of change is so rapidly accelerated in the past few years that we cannot keep up with it, it is absolutely imperative that there be women in all crucial situations, women in the legal system, in the medical system, in all the places that can somehow or other move the political system, because if not, something is going to be very much lacking in the resolution of these global difficulties and problems.

There is a different and new kind of challenge than has ever existed before in our society. It is one that calls for all of us, men and women, to educate ourselves constantly and continuously to be competent and equal to the tasks of discussion, decision-making, and action. It demands mutual listening, consideration of options, alternatives, and new possibilities.

Antoine St. Exupéry, in a beautiful book called "The Citadel," makes this statement: "Women have a repugnance for the purely expedient and for whatever smacks of totalitarianism."[6] He may simply have been making an existential observation: that women react against anything that is totalitarian, that they are not so terribly pragmatic. This is not to say that no man possesses the same traits. But, if women possess those traits in great degree, then they serve to remind men that strength, real strength, is not in aggression but in self-possession, that there is a manly gentleness and compassion that can divert humanity from war. That gentleness is not something to be ashamed of. That work and leisure can both be fuller, warmer, and less rigid. that power can be "nonviolent." That peace *is* possible.

Basically, the cause of freeing woman from past attitudes which have not kept pace with the rest of evolutionary development can never be moved forward by argumentation that sees woman only as a wounded victim. Men and women both have been victimized by culture, by society and multiple historical structures. The human molecule is the most complex organism on the planet and needs to be understood in all it complexity. Differences should be celebrated because differences are by no means defects. The humanization and personalization that is hoped for demands that differences be seen in a correlative, relational, reciprocal and real mutuality, as the means for uniting humankind.

> True union does not confound: it differentiates and personalizes. A principle entirely simple but capable, if well understood, of placing us in a new world.[7]

Chapter 3 will examine the concepts of Secularity and Stewardship as expressions of personal responsibility in a new world.

[6] Antoine de St. Exupéry, *The Citadel* (Paris: Editions Gallimard, 1948), passim.

[7] Teilhard de Chardin, "Pour y voir clair," *Les Etudes Philosophiques,* 10 (1955), 575.

Our past is not our potential.
In any hour, with all the stubborn
teachers and healers of history who
called us to our best selves, we
can liberate the future. One by one we
can rechoose to awaken, to leave
the prison of our conditioning,
                                    to love
to turn homeward.
To *conspire* with and for each other.
Awakening brings its own assignments,
    Unique to each of us,
    chosen by each of us,
Whatever you may think about yourself,
    and however long you may have thought it,
    you are not just you.
You are a seed, a silent promise.

Marilyn Ferguson,
Aquarian Conspiracy

3

The Challenge: Creative Responsibility

"Then God said ... have dominion over all the earth, ...
and over every living thing that moves upon the earth."
Genesis 1:26,28.

Stewardship of Planet Earth

This scriptural reference introduces the questions emerging
from a contemporary view of Creation, and invites a searching
answer. Human activity is necessary; the work is love; the
"dominion" is reconciliation; the message is hope.

From the world of molecular biologists to that of nuclear
physicists and astronomers, we are daily reminded of the
galactic changes that the earth is presently undergoing.
Quasars, black holes, and stars whose light is only now beginning to reach us are realities and events with which the youn-
gest school child will soon be comfortably familiar. The
discovery of an incredibly bright quasar (a star-like body the
size of the solar system) 100,000 billion times brighter than the
sun, the most distant object in the sky (roughly 90 percent of
the way to the edge of the universe) is a perfect example of the
awesome dimensions of our universe. Although its light has
taken 13 billion years to reach earth, the quasar probably no

longer even exists. Even more interesting, scientists are attempting to show that all known forces in the universe derive from a single force—the force religious believers have always named as God, now seen as God of evolution, of cosmogenesis. The vast sweep of evolution raises a myriad of questions about the origins of the universe, to be sure, but what is most significant is the growing realization that the human component of this incredible dynamic sphere called earth really is spinning in a space-ship, with second-by-second decisions to be made about its future. Once this is internalized, once we realize that we are all part of the one same reality, all vitally linked to each other, no matter on what part of this tiny globe we live, then common effort to carve out solutions to our multiplying problems will replace atomized efforts to seek superiority over the other. It is here that the concept of mutuality continues to provide us with a framework. Mutuality encompasses unconditional love, and allows for each partner in the union to bring to bear all of her/his gifts to any situation, and to have those gifts acknowledged, as well as to have one's own personal needs met. If we begin with the thought that God needs us in order for creation to continue, we immediately sense not only our responsibility, but our worth, our value in the scheme of things. Creation has moved arduously and over billions of years, to the point where reflective humans are free to choose to love, to be mutual with the mysterious Creator. The possibility of reflective human beings choosing not to love, not to be mutual, is also actualized all around us. It is not difficult to discover many who seem incapable of loving, of allowing themselves the risk of vulnerability. Even worse, we are confronted with individuals and institutions in which the choice for evil finds deliberate embodiment. Where is there room for hope in such a world? In the symbolic novel, *The Plague,* Albert Camus' hero muses that "the plague had robbed us all of the capacity for love, and even friendship, for LOVE requires a little future."[1] It is this belief in a future that

---

[1]Camus Albert, *The Plague,* trans. Stuart Gilbert (New York: Modern Library, 1948) 169.

can enkindle love, and with it an unassailable hope against hope even when faced with the stark evidence of evil in our midst. It is this kind of loving hope that enables persons to be creative in their personal lives and relationships, and to extend that hope and creativity to the societal and global situation.

But can such hope long survive without the encouraging support that comes from sharing those hopes and beliefs? It cannot. And that is why we now see so many groupings, associations, and international movements that are dedicated to human need. These are not isolated phenomena, but rather they represent a phase of evolutionary growth of a vanguard of people who have understood the concept of mutual inter-dependence. For example, one of the most creative responses to the African famine in 1986 was sparked by a group of entertainers. It was a basically religious response which employed the best of technology to unite people all over the world—first in song, then in concrete action. It was liturgy in the finest sense of that word, a secular Eucharist which effected what it signified. Such an event could only transpire in a world which over the centuries had been celebrating and professing that kind of love in small groups. The diffusion of that creative spirit which will renew the face of the earth was enhanced by modern transportation and communication, to be sure, but it had been carried to all parts of the world in word and deed long before Live-Aid. So it is with other movements of liber-ation. The very first creation story, we have seen, emerged from a liberating experience—the Exodus. The primitive Semites who composed the Genesis version of creation did so out of the profound experience that the one who had saved their lives was one and the same with the one who had given them life. Creation and liberation go hand-in-hand. If we are beginning to see a new freedom for all persons, regardless of color or race, or sex, it is not because they were not always created equal, but because in an evolutionary forward thrust, we are finally beginning to hear the word of creation. The century in which we find ourselves is one in which the pace of evolution has so rapidly accelerated that it encompasses all of the advances of all of the centuries before it. It is small wonder that we have come to better understand the sameness and differentiation of the human molecule. What is evident in all of evolution becomes specified at the human level as "individuation" in Carl Jung's terms. Our next step is to genuinely recognize the implications of that understanding for decision-making in government, medicine, the legal system, international relations—in every area where women and men work together. Highly individuated, ever-more conscious persons will push the process.

Persons In Process, A World In Motion

It is here then that we will introduce a contemporary theological framework, one on which to build a personal synthesis between this expressed faith and contemporary culture. The theological framework based on the scriptural is ordered toward the pastoral. Within such a frame of reference, the concepts of Process, Person, and Secularization are suggested as being essential to contemporary discussion of Creation and creative responsibility. Following upon that, our reflection will lead us to the themes of relationality, mutuality, and friendship, with their implications for personal, societal, and global communities.

Process, persons, and a world of matter and Spirit still in the process of becoming—in such a rapidly evolving universe of persons, what does it mean to be fully human? Is it an art? Or is it, as Teilhard de Chardin says, "a thirst for self-achievement and an attraction toward an absolute?" Is it finding the self in one's own depths as Jung would have it, or reaching self-actualization through peak experiences in the famous model of Abraham Maslow? It is *all* this—and more. No other century has been faced with the question of what it means to be a human person, a female person, a male person, in precisely the way this twentieth century has. The questions are different, precisely because of the other two factors involved—the evolutionary process, and a deeper grasp of the significance of matter, of the very earth we inhabit, of the sacredness of the secular.

As humanity has evolved and changed, so too has its self-understanding and relation to the world changed. The possibilities for creative transformation of persons, for incorporating both the pain and suffering, and also an abiding hope that extends into a more human future are open and beckoning. Contemporary literature, science, art, theology, music, psychology—all have the potential for revealing more about what it is to be a whole person. These human "disciples" emphasize that union is better than isolation, to be sure, but more than that, they state unequivocally that to be in relationship is *constitutive* of being human. A sense of organic wholeness, a realization that we are all part of a whole is the "feel" for the truly human. Using the concepts of person, process, and secularization, then, we will again recall the "law" of complexity-consciousness with its corollary that union differentiates, for the implications these ideas have for the achievement of personhood in community through mutuality. Hopefully, these prior insights, infused as they are by an authentic religious conviction about the ultimacy of human life, will lead to a broadening of our understanding of the human process in all of its multi-faceted dimensions, and so to a deeper understanding of the newness of the project in this century for women and men seeking mutuality.

If humanization is a process, it is a process that seeks to be rooted and grounded in *hope*. Of necessity, it must also be a process of relationing, relationing that goes beyond the personal to the societal, the global, and the cosmic. This evolutionary point of view, which contemporary persons can ignore only to their own loss, is expressive of humanity as evolution conscious of itself, pressing forward.

Some of the further implications and ramifications of the scientific evolutionary thought that permeate our thinking and acting are our awareness that nothing remains stationary, that the future already impinges on our present. Not to go forward is to regress, and as human consciousness continues to grow, personal responsibility for creating that future which "is already but not yet" increases.

In this evolving universe of persons (which is the only

universe we experience), the significance of person has likewise been born anew. From philosophical and psychological vantage points, we are constantly reminded that person is the prime value, that humanity thirsts for personalization. The deeper internationalization of the concept of person as unique, full of mystery, full of dignity, full of potential, complex, existing as dyad, is taking place all around us within a human vanguard. Interlocking with this emphasis on person is the process of taking the secular or "world" seriously—not so seriously that we think that the world is all there is, but so seriously that we acknowledge its created goodness, and its need for responsible stewards. Secularization is not secularism, but rather a process reactive to sacralism, which tended to separate humanity from that personal Mystery which is as immanent as it is transcendent. In the final analysis, sacralism obscures the primacy and mystery of person just as much as unmitigated secularism does. Secularization, on the other hand, strips away obstacles and artificiality, revealing history and relationships at their deepest levels.

Whenever and wherever we find a reconciliation of the seeming opposition between sacred and secular, between community and person, accompanied by a growing taste for and love of the earth, there we touch on *le sens humain,* the feel for the human whole. It goes without saying that such faith and hope in the world and in the future of the human endeavor rest on an unassailable hope in an Absolute Future. Is there a paradigm for a faith that is total risk, the hope that will not be quenched, the love that sets neither limit nor condition? Individually, we cannot be the answers to our own questions and fears. We are afraid of the dead-end-no-future; we are afraid of not being loved; we are afraid of having no one to believe in and even worse, no one to believe in us.

The movement, then, must be toward the mystery of love itself, of friendship, of union. True union, we have already noted, does not confound. It differentiates and personalizes. A principle entirely simple, but capable—if well understood—of placing before us a new world.

Initially, this statement of differentiating union reminds us that the human molecule which we are is the most complex organism alive. Next, we recalled that this human molecule exists dyadically, not as a monad. It is wholly composed of male and female components, able to come together in unity precisely because they are in some respects exquisitely different, both in "withoutness" and "withinness," complexity and consciousness.

In such a process of differentiating union, personal identity is not lost, the self is not assimilated or obliterated by the other, but, on the contrary, the *sine qua non* for union and growth is differentiation. Uniqueness is not only recognized, it is demanded. this personal reality is, in fact, a principle that can be extended and applied at four levels.

The first level is the cosmic. The cosmos is able to be called to union with God precisely because the world is not God and God is not the world. It is for this reason that we can speak of the mystery of God as being "mutual" with the world. The differentiation and integration of the created order has been taking place slowly since its inception. The movement has been from chaos toward order, from lesser organisms toward higher, through suffering, evil, pain and beauty. The universe is straining not to *become* God but to be *at one* with God. This is not a pantheism, but a pan-en-theism. Such a cosmos needs compassion from the human persons who are part of it. Even before looking at the compassion that we need for each other, a growing awareness of our relationship to the earth is of singular importance.

The next level is societal. At this level, we need to look to differentiation as it applies to relationships that have to do with recognizing the sovereignty of various cultures, the distinctions between races, the causes of injustice, the questions of compassionate alternatives concerning war and peace, poverty and wealth, inequitable distribution of goods, the quality of life itself. The quest for the specific temporal betterment of all persons in society is based upon our common humanity, but it must take seriously our differences which are not defects. Much of liberation theology derives not only from its emphasis on the humanity of Jesus, but also on its awareness of the principle of differentiation as being a main factor in speaking about human equality.

The third and fourth levels, the personal and the communal, cannot be looked at separately, since they are linked in reality, as well as structurally. They are not polarities; they are more than correlatives.

We have reached a point where our technology has enabled us to split the nucleus of the atom, to unravel the whole process of fusion, to abort the entire human/earth project. What is absolutely essential then is that we raise up women and men whose wisdom and compassion will not allow us to do this. Thus, the very first implication of a Christian evolutionary theory of Creation is that God, the Mystery at the heart of the process, leaves us free to be responsible for the way the process will continue. While the Mystery is ultimately and necessarily the dynamic cause of the process, human cooperation is also necessary, if not sufficient, in order for evil to be diminished and alleviated. Once this notion is grasped, then areas of human activity which may not have seemed particularly "religious" or "sacred" become absolutely so. Ecology, race relations, the way in which women and men live and work together are significant concerns, not only for prayer, but for responsible action. To impress this on the hearts of people who have long lived with the idea that religion is about "holy rituals" alone is the task of the contemporary Church. Human beings who have considered "morality" to be concerned only with personal sexual behavior are called to understand that political ethics, honesty in dealing with the public, accurate advertising through all-powerful forms of media, nuclear policy, world hunger, educational priorities, are the significant and genuine moral issues, sacred issues, religious issues.

Sacred and Secular: Inextricably Linked

Understanding the human person to be a free and creative agent, we look, in life, for those persons and situations which will enhance freedom and creativity. An emphasis on faith and hope in the future of the human endeavor rests in unassailable hope in an absolute future as that hope is embodied in Christ. If God is for us, who can be against us? But Christ was for God in a kind of mutuality that is also asked of us. He was "for God" by being "for us" and we can only be "for God" by being for each other and for the world. "Incarnation" is a continuation of a process, a process of mutuality, which lends dignity to our humanness once we have grasped it. The notion of mutuality definitely applies to our concepts of God, concepts which for too long placed God apart from us, totally transcendent, as if we were merely accessory or ancillary to the human project. Such a supposition placed the whole responsibility for all that happens squarely on the One called God, and gave us a *deus ex machina.* It did not give us Jeremiah's Jahweh; it did not give us the Jahweh of Abraham, of Isaac. It did not give us the nurturing parent, the Abba of Jesus Christ. Rather, it offered an image, impersonal and totally apart from anything that we experience when we truly experience relationality. One of the most poignant and extraordinary presentations of such an uninvolved God is given in the novel *The Color Purple,* by Alice Walker (who won a Pulitzer prize for writing it, but who deserves a prize for all of us for demanding that we examine our own "god images"). The mutuality that she allows one of her characters to experience with all of creation is descriptive of the most classic of mystical experiences. After almost convincing her companion, Celie, that God could not possibly be a larger than life Caucasian male, Shug goes on to tell her of her own real experience of God as Spirit.

> Here's the thing, say Shug. The thing I believe. God is inside you and inside everybody else. You come into the world with God. But only them that search for it inside find it. And sometimes it just manifest itself even if you not looking, or don't know what you looking for. . . .
> My first step away from the old white man was trees. Then air. Then birds. Then other people. But one day when I was

sitting quiet and feeling like a motherless child, which I was, it come to me: that feeling of being part of everything, not separate at all. I knew that if I cut a tree, my arm would bleed. And I laughed and I cried and I ran all around the house. . . .

She finishes by telling Celie that whenever she tries to pray, and that old white man "plop himself on the other end of it, tell him to git lost. Conjure up flowers, wind, water, a big rock."[2] Wind, water, rock, my fortress, a mother with her child, a spouse to a beloved, a hen with chickens—so many beautiful images to choose from—none of them "enough", not one to be preferred. The writer Annie Dillard in describing her own religious experience ended up calling the Mystery of God the Holy, the Firm. That images of the immense God of the Universe be enlarged beyond any traditional restrictive male images is an imperative well-recognized by anyone seriously examining the theological implications of the evolutionary world-view.

For the modern believer, this existential "God experience" becomes a question about the possible coincidence—or on the other hand—absence of coherence between faith in the world of persons and human endeavor, and faith in a Christ who is of God. How to live in faith, hope, and love? How to be human in a less than human world? Are faith, hope, and love "virtues," separated from the human endeavor? Or are they truly attitudinal aspects that belong to a new humanness, born out of all that is really human?

The relationship that is coercive, the relationship that is authoritarian, the relationship that is manipulative (however subtle) is not human relationship. So, whether in the close, intimate relationships of marriage or friendship, or societal relationships, or those with the world, when a person becomes "objectified" or reduced to an "it", or when persons and

---

[2]Alice Walker, *The Color Purple*, (New York: Washington Square Press, 1982) 175-179.

relationships lose reality (to borrow from Martin Buber's language "if they are no longer a 'thou' for us"), there can be no more personal development. The search for personhood is aborted, or at least diminished. To the degree that we depersonalize or dehumanize any person who touches our life, to that same degree, and *more so,* are we diminished.

Many notions of process have been placed before us. There is, of course, an opposing viewpoint, strongly Aristotelian and even Thomistic, that "things have been this way forever, and they will always be this way." But, in point of fact, we know that we are in constant process. We are dynamic. we cannot stand still. Not to go forward is to regress. Not to change, move, and develop is to go backwards, because we can't stand still.

Everyone who lives in the twentieth century is, in reality, a "process philosopher," whether consciously acknowledged or not. We may try to stifle that notion of process, and cling to past formulations somewhere in some part of our brain. However, our observations of a constantly changing universe are themselves subject to change and modification. Even evolution is evolving! What once was seen as "natural selection" in pre-human species, no longer applies because human reflection, as we very well know can alter processes, change genetic coding, hopefully conquer death-dealing diseases. But when we ask if there is a future, and whether we believe in the future, and whether we believe the future will be better, we proceed on the basis and assumption of hope— *hope,* not optimism, because there is nothing to be optimistic about.

When we internalize that notion and realize the challenge before us, we are enabled to change and re-think positions that we may have held firmly in the past. We become vulnerable. If we so change, we must then invite other people into those same vulnerable positions. The implications and the ramifications of this idea of process flow over into every area of our lives.

The process of secularization, which takes place in this real world that we talk about, is not something to be thought of as an evil or a negative. It is simply reality. The world around us is evolving, and we are part of that development. Yet we are at the critical threshold where we are being asked whether or not we will go forward in union, in love, in community, or whether we will be stymied by fear. Will we go backwards because we allow love to be undone? In other words, do we set up enmities and hatreds by default because of fear to love?

We live on a very small planet. We live on a planet in which we are discovering more and more about the human brain. We live on a planet in which we realize that we are called to be co-creators. We are called to be the healers of this global village which is wounded and fragmented. We are called to look upon this small spinning sphere and become aware of our common home. We are coming closer at this point in history to understanding the phrase, Family of God, as the whole human family.

The notion that this Earth requires our stewardship is a basic religious notion, and we are no longer able to compartmentalize life by agreeing to tend to our own little corner of the Earth. Planet Earth is our home, and we share it with the billions of people who inhabit it. We all have the same fears and anxieties. We have the same kind of common fears about being able to preserve that world; and about whether or not the vision of peace, which is the eschatological vision of all religious peoples, is something that is still very far away from us.

The underlying premise in all that we have been discussing is that our present view of Creation demands human response. The planet needed persons whose consciousness can keep pace with the increased complexity of our technology. Ecological disasters, genetic engineering, distribution of wealth, disarmament are all theological issues, the stuff of prayer. How to achieve such mature faith is a question that confronts us all. Mature faith that becomes convinced action gives meaning to the phrase "seeing God in all things." This phrase has long been ascribed to Ignatius of Loyola as the basis of Christian spirituality. It typifies, still, the best of contemporary spirituality, with its accompanying emphasis on contemplation in action. Both are of absolute importance. In the present historical period, many questions that once seemed to have solid, unequivocal answers now seem to warrant options, alternatives. Authentic resolution of current ethical dilemmas calls for informed and educated people, who see this as a new horizon of religious activity. A "creative transformation of human history," as Jurgen Moltmann's puts it, is another way of talking about salvation.

We are presented with the possibility of speaking more positively about actively diminishing evil, rather than concentration on expiation or individual reparation as leading to "salvation."

> A collective optimism, realistic and courageous, must without any doubt take the place of the individualism and pessimisms whose exaggerated ideas of sin and personal salvation have gradually infiltrated and distorted the Christian spirit.[3]

The reformulation of the doctrine of original sin, as suggested by Teilhard, and followed through by Piet Schoonenberg, Piet Smulders, Bernard Haring and others opens doors for a new understanding of soteriology, in which the human community must assume its dignity and responsibility for diminishing evil. Evil is seen in both its physical and moral dimensions as a statistical inevitability in a world which is incomplete. The misplaced question of its "origins" properly shift to the necessity of human engagement in diminishing evil wherever it is found.

There is no question but that we are at a critical point in human evolution, wherein our immersion into the human project must be our expression of our faith in creation. Decisions to confront the catastrophes that surround us will make persons more responsible. Imaginative and creative responses

---

[3]Teilhard de Chardin, "Reflections on Original Sin," *Christianity and Evolution* (New York: Harcourt Brace, Jovanovich, 1969) 186.

will require a more practical asceticism. Awareness that matter and spirit inform each other will make the "corporal and spiritual works of mercy" the agenda for all humanity. The message of the Beatitudes takes on global significance. The concept of a "divine milieu" presents us with the possibility of seeing ourselves more clearly as "divine/ human persons" who are called to do God's work, holding a common hope. The most pressing "works of God" which demand cohesion and solidarity are world hunger and poverty, the struggle for peace and racial equality. A new theology of creation demands response.

World Hunger: The Cry of the Poor

In 1985, 512 million people were hungry in developing countries, and almost half were children. While the majority of hungry people still live in Asia and Africa, even in the most highly industrialized country in the world (USA), 20 million people are hungry at least twice a month. In the last decade, since 1980, the number of hungry people in the U.S. has increased dramatically. The tragedy of all this is that hunger *could* end in this century, but its causes are too deeply rooted in unjust economic structures. So there is a definite correlation between greed and affluence and the poverty that is a primary cause of world hunger.

Another major factor contributing to world hunger is the disproportionate rate of military spending world-wide. The relationship between personal morality and opinion on this issue and active engagement as an expression of faith is central. Poor people need education, health care, jobs in a stable economy. If systemic oppression of the poor is to be eliminated, individuals have to use their influence politically to change governments' policies and priorities. The private sector needs to push the public sector, because private contributions and personal charity are not enough to solve the problem.

"One stroke of the President's pen or one vote by Congress can have a positive impact on hungry people that dwarfs private efforts on their behalf."[4] The admirable work being

---

[4]Margaret Mead, *New York Times*, December 1968.

done by committed groups such as Bread for the World, Catholic Relief Services, Jesuit Relief Services, Save The Children, and many, many others is insufficient to transform the present crisis. Unfortunately, there are voices which, while claiming to honor the Judaeo-Christian tradition, nevertheless decry efforts to relieve poverty through redistribution of human resources. These are the pathetic voices that solemnly intone that "the poor are poor because they choose to be," that "street people live on the street because they like it," and all the other "justifications" for doing nothing. This self-righteous position ignores the impact of the gospel message: "I was hungry and you did not feed me." To be moved from such attitudes, people must really be convinced that their communion must find expression in breaking bread with God's poor.

In Philadelphia, one small boy, Trevor Farrell, seeing people starving and shivering on the streets, began a ministry to the homeless which has grown incredibly. This is a simple example of the compassion of one person influencing others to acts of self-renunciation and gratitude. It is important, and yet it must be followed through by political action.

It is a critical dimension of aid to the poor that it be personal, and that it preserve their dignity by encouraging those living in poverty to become more productive. The international group known as the Fourth World Movement, works to bring awareness of the very poor living in the midst of plenty in the ghettoes of major cities worldwide.

The new human spirit finds expression in aid to the disadvantaged no matter what country they inhabit. What is especially new about it is that it is no longer just bureaucratic institutionalized "foreign aid," but rather people to people assistance. The brilliant and sensitive Margaret Mead foresaw the significance of this when she wrote in the New York Times in December 1968: "A nation that refuses to grow food where food is needed, and refuses to give of its abundance to those who are starving, wherever they are, becomes a nation insensitive to the needs of its own people. To cherish our own, we must do our full part in helping to care for the world."[5]

[5]Ibid.

Peace-Making: The Miracle to Come

Faith in peace and its possibility is a strong theme in the thought of Teilhard de Chardin. He bases his hopes on evolution itself, and the modern advances in transportation and communication on a sphere. By reason of the fact that the human community is linked genetically in its origins, and interrelated by the very shape of the globe, he sees peace coming about out of sheer necessity. "Humanity is not only capable of living in peace, but by its very structure cannot fail eventually to achieve peace." A "sustained stage of growing convergence and concentration, a great organized endeavor ..." this is peace. The efforts that are taking place on the planet at this time are hints and pointers that this instinct for unification is being realized among those who have achieved high levels of consciousness. Shall we have compression with fear (Cold War), or convergence through love (international cooperation)?

The summits between the two ideologically opposed superpowers in December 1987 in Washington, D.C. and in Moscow in 1988, have sparked hope in the hearts of many, and brought some consolation to those who have been struggling and protesting within the Peace Movement. The women of southern England, the "greens" of West Germany, the "Berrigans" of the world, and thousands of nameless others felt somewhat vindicated and encouraged. Peace-making is hard work, but in a true evolutionary pattern, "everything that once made for war now makes for peace, and the zoological laws of conservation and survival must wear an opposite sign if they are to be applied to humanity."[6]

This is true because of the *particular* and *unique* structure of the zoological group to which we belong:

> Until the coming Man, the branches or shoots composing the different living species tended inexorably to diverge and

---

[6]Teilhard de Chardin, "Faith in Peace," *The Future of Man,* (New York: Harper and Row, 1947) 155.

spread ever more widely apart as they developed. With
Man, on the other hand, moving to the grand psychological
phenomenon of Reflection, the branches of this species
follow an entirely different course. Instead of separating
and detaching themselves from one another they turn
inwards and presently intertwine, so that by degrees, races,
peoples, nations merging together, they come to form a sort
of uni-conscious super-organism.[7]

The whole of the essay "Faith in Peace" is vibrant with a great
hope, born of biological certainty, that "the earth is more
likely to stop turning than is Mankind, as a whole, likely to
stop organizing and unifying itself." The disruptive forces at
work in the world are a kind of last gasp of diminished forces
struggling against something which is emerging from the
depths of the human spirit. To achieve Peace, we must ascend
a steep slope, but ultimately we will, as a whole, achieve a
balance point. This peace so long dreamed of is not to be
conceived of as "bourgeois tranquility," or worse, "millenary
felicity." This would not be coherent with an advancing universe in tense cohesion. But rather, peace can be envisioned as
a struggle for greater consciousness and freedom. In this
struggle, the energy wasted in bloodshed would be shifted to
the conquest of life's difficulties, the sublimation of warfare.
For this to happen we must look beyond the demonstrations
for peace and even conscientious objection to war—however
important these are—to the constitutional determination to
search for *knowledge* that will help to achieve the true fulfillment of human power and destiny. This, then will create a
truly new Spirit of humanity, a spirit of peace.

Ecology and Planetary Survival

Some of the most significant contributions to understanding
the ecological period in which we find ourselves come from

7Ibid.

the writings of Thomas Berry. For more than a decade, Berry, a theologian of world religions and of a "theology of the earth," has contributed greatly to the work begun by Rachel Carson in *Silent Spring*. The climatic changes that we observe as a result of what has been termed the greenhouse effect will surely increase famine and bring about social disruptions of an incredible magnitude. Meeting with international scientists in Toronto, American biologists Ann and Paul Ehrlich have pointed out the results of our continued burning of fossil fuels. The carbon dioxides emitted are literally changing the climate, warming the earth by destroying the "good" ozone layer. What is sure to be effected early in the next century is starting right now. The sulfur oxides also produce the acid rains that are destroying our forests. The pollution of the seas has gone so far as to be irreversible in the thought of many who examine the problem internationally. Raw sewage, hospital wastes illegally dumped, trash transported from one country to another—almost always to the poorest of the poor countries— are killing the marine life in our oceans and bays. This destruction of valuable sources of food further depletes the limited resources needed to alleviate world poverty. While millions of concerned people all over the world decry the irresponsibility and criminal neglect, others seem bent on ignoring impending doom and even profiting from some of the root causes. The necessity of those who are "more human," more conscious, prevailing over the less highly evolved, in terms of planetary consciousness, is all too evident.

That such a spirit could develop systematically is dependent upon the individual and personal awareness of what it means to be more human, and that our humanity is completely inter-dependent with that of everyone else. This thought has been repeated many times throughout these reflections, and it is as basic to a Christian understanding of what it is to be human as it is to any biological and humanistic understandings. The logical, though not inevitable, conclusion of these reflections on creation is that the human community has both an obli-gation and a need to set priorities. It is not that certain values are mutually exclusive, but that some values are more signi-ficant than others. The problems of nuclear weapons, world hunger, apartheid and all other forms of repression emerge as the pivotal redemptive questions. Other issues within a creation ethic must ultimately be weighed against these global realities. For example, we have looked at the relationship between the sexes, and the need for a liberating new understanding of that relationship. It is important, however, not to confuse the question as it exists in pluralistic free societies with the oppression that exists in third and fourth world situations, where even children are unjustly imprisoned and tortured. While powerful people argue the wisdom of proliferating nuclear stockpiles or proposing war in space, problems within the Churches concerning progressive and conservative positions must take second place surely. What is being looked for is an expansion of horizons, a true evolution of human consciousness to global concern. The "human front" knows no national boundaries. Its concerns for the future are cosmic, and this sense is in perfect conformity with the geographic contraction that is taking place through mass media and instant transportation with the accompanying psychological compression. Combined efforts in research, based on hope for the future of the entire universe will be seen to replace the priorities of isolated nations. Technology must be put at the service of humanization. Sincere and convinced artisans of progress will emerge as this growing humanization process continues. The very technological development that surrounds us on all sides is an awakening of spirit in the world. Advances in technology represent an increase in complexity, and are meant to be accompanied by a psychic, spiritual progress, an increase in human freedom and responsibility that represents a correlative in consciousness. This is, of course, a major problem when questions of medical ethics, such as those concerned with embryology, organ transplants and prolongation of life are raised.

Just as our views on all reality have been stretched, likewise the role of the Christ needs to be seen in an expanded view, which is also global and universal, not restricted in time or place, or to any one church. Chapter 4 will look at these questions as they are inextricably bound up with our ideas of Creation and Redemption.

The Lord created me at the beginning of God's works,
before all else that the Lord made, long ago.
Alone, I was fashioned in times long past,
at the beginning, long before the earth itself.
When there was yet no ocean I was born,
no springs brimming with water.
Before the mountains were settled in their place,
long before hills I was born,
when as yet the Lord had made neither land nor lake
nor the first clod of earth.
When God set the heavens in their place I was there,
when God girdled the ocean with the horizon,
when God fixed the canopy of clouds overhead
and set the springs of ocean firm in their place,
when the Lord prescribed its limits for the sea
and knit together earth's foundation.
Then I was at the Lord's side each day,
God's darling and delight,
playing in God's presence continually,
playing on the earth, when the Lord had finished it,
while my delight was in all of humanity.

                                                    Proverbs 8:22-31

4

The Word and Hope: The Christological Dimension

"God so loved the world that He gave his only begotten Son to the end that those who believe in him should not die but have everlasting life."

(John 3:16)

The Christological dimension of this contemporary study of Creation with which we began is paramount. Following the evolutionary model, it becomes apparent that the entrance of the Christ into humanity in the individual person of Jesus of Nazareth marked a critical threshold, a change in the sphere as great as the movements from non-living matter to life, and from life to reflective life. "The beginning of God's works, God's darling and delight" found his own delight in the world of human persons. It is necessary to ask what it means to say that there was fullness of the divine/human communion in the man Jesus. We must also ask how our human understanding of the Christ and his relationship to the whole of creation, not just the earth, but the universe, has changed. Our new understanding of the earth, ourselves, and the challenges earth offers affect this understanding. As God has immersed herself/himself in Creation through the emergence of Jesus from within the human family, we see humanity now clearly called to continue that divine life. Jesus, God's man, the person of unconditional love, full of compassion, always forgiving and unafraid, is the very Christ who is at the heart of creation, who gathers up all of creation. Since Christ is the term of evolution, since the world can no more have two centers than a circumference can have two centers, evolution itself is holy, and what might have been seen as irreconcilable—faith in the world and the human, and faith in a God—can no longer be seen in that light.

Following the law of complexity-consciousness, one can say that it is the whole human community that is to be "Christified," called to a new spiritual awakening, a higher raising of consciousness not quite possible before a certain passage of time. With the exception of those human persons of all great religions who lived the life of the Spirit so intensely that they were called mystics, the "sancti", the potential for allowing the Christ-consciousness to emerge in everyone has not been fully realized. Contemporary awareness of the human role in the universe is bringing about a totally new awareness of Christ in Creation as embodied in the whole of the human community.

Reflecting on the Johannine message that "God so loved the world that He gave his only begotten Son to the end that those who believe in him should not die but have everlasting life" (Jn 3:16), theologian John Yungblut suggests that these words must be transposed "into a new Key, resonant to and harmonious with the fresh revelation we have received in our twentieth century via the discovery of evolution and the perspective of depth psychology." He continues, "A new statement of our central Christ myth, allowed to evolve that it might acquire fresh vitality in our day, would run something like this:

> God so loved the world that God implanted deeply and darkly in matter itself the seed that, through continuing Creation by evolution, would one day bear fruit in the Christ-life of other men and women to their ultimate fulfillment and salvation.[1]

[1]John Yungblut, essay in *American Teilhard de Chardin Newsletter, 5, 1988.*

This transposition into a new key is what another American theologian, John Dwyer, calls for when he examines the problems of traditional Christological understandings. Dwyer points out that the language we use concerning the Christ is frequently language we do not understand, which does not address the current world situation and the meaning of Christ in such a world. He urges a return to the Scriptural language, reminding us that the New Testament only provides "sketches and proposals" about Jesus "rather than concepts which would actually succeed in holding him."[2] He urges that we decode and embrace the symbols of religious language, and it would seem that John Yungblut has done just that. Dwyer finally invites us to reflect on the power of the world itself to speak to us of God, and our own power to find in the human reality and human personhood of Jesus Christ, the human face of God.[3]

Remembering that Paul was the first person to use human language in an attempt to express the mystery of God in Christ, we can see the idea of "sketchy proposals" quite clearly. Paul's efforts were *so* tentative!

In the epistle to the Romans, Paul's own groping for a proposition results in his telling us that God ordained that "his own"—you, me, all of us—"should be shaped to the likeness of his son, that he might be the eldest among a large family of brothers and sisters. There is nothing that can separate us from that love—nothing in all creation—nothing except our own refusal to love—"for to those who love God and are called in God's name everything works out for good." (Rom 8:28,29,39)

Later, when Paul writes to the Christians at Corinth, he writes about reconciliation and our part in the process. He will continue the paradigm of the direct relationship between Christ, Creation, and the human community:

[2]John Dwyer, "Theoretical Linguistics and the Problems of Christology," *Catholic Theological Proceedings* (vol. 40, 1987), 16, passim.
[3]Ibid.

> From the first to last this has been the work of God. He has
> reconciled us to himself through Christ, and has enlisted us
> in this service of reconciliation. What I mean is: *God was in*
> *Christ reconciling the world to himself . . .* he has entrusted
> us with the message of reconciliation. (2 Cor 5:18-20)

This is the essential meaning of the Christian phenomenon.
Growing within the human phylum as a "replica" of it,
Christianity maintains its axial position precisely as the phylum
of love and reconciliation directing human psychic energy.
Christianity holds the key to man's evolutionary progress, not
only because it fulfills the criteria of productivity and coherence
demanded by a world-view, but more especially because it can
do so through Love. It is meant to be engaged in the service of
reconciliation, reconciling all that is broken, fragmented, alien-
ated.

Love can be achieved precisely because of its ability to
personalize according to the principle that union differentiates.
The necessity of humanity's seeking this union, attempting to
overcome divergence, separation, alienation, individualism, is
paramount. If ever the human community were to be convinced that true union does differentiate, that it is a function of
personalization, then all would exercise their own unique
creative abilities in union with others regardless of function.
With love as the source and reason for living, people would be
compelled to take part in "all the anxieties, all the aspirations,
all the affections of the earth, insofar as these embody a principle of *ascension* and *synthesis.*[4]

That the scientific model previously examined is consistent
and coherent with the most recent exegetical interpretation
becomes clear. That each approach, the scriptural and the
scientific/speculative, is indispensable for the development of
a new anthropology and Christology is already clear. Contemporary language about the vast processes involved in evolution is rich and exciting. Scriptural language about Christ and

---

[4]Thomas Berry, "Christian Humanism," Riverdale Papers II (Riverdale, NY 1979).

human possibilities is rich and simple, with the richness of mysticism, and the simplicity of metaphor and simile. (One of the richest images is, of course, the continually developing body of Christ theme, in all its unique newness in the thought of Paul.)

Running beside these contemporary reflections on the cosmic Christ of St. Paul is another important contribution from Thomas Berry. He calls for new religious orientations, a new phase of religious awareness. He foresees religions converging upon each other, as they engage more and more in the earth-human process."[5] But now are we to interpret the New Testament presentation, with its somatic understanding of a cosmic Christ, and relate it to the earth-human process as a paradigm? Only by affirming the Chalcedon formula with a presently deepened understanding of the earliest Christian witness. Looking for Paul's "ripe-time" for the revelation of human relationing in the mystery of God, we are confronted with an immense challenge. How does the Jesus/Christ event affect the human effort to become more human?

A growing ability to perceive more deeply the whole mystery of Jesus as affecting human life radically is in accord with the law of complexity/consciousness. It is not insignificant that as we gradually come to know more about ourselves, we can correspondingly know more about the meaning of Jesus, the Christ. Together with the gradual, objective unfolding of the complexities of teachings about him, that is, the expanding of theological horizons, the human capacity for "sight" has also expanded. Through a direct evolutionary process of growth, it seems logical to say that human persons can know more about the significance of Christ. Conversely and correlatively, knowing more about the man Jesus can only help us to know more about what it means to be human in the fullest sense. In a cosmos in which there is always more "to be seen," the human person concomitantly develops better "eyes" for seeing. This "seeing" is a new step in evolution, an act of amorization:

seeing more and more deeply means being able to love the mystery of life more deeply.

> Through the living tradition of a faith and a mystique, the Christian organism diffuses or expresses in itself an ever more awakened sense of Christ present and active *in the fulfillments of the world.* We cannot continue to love Christ without discovering him more and more.[6]

The evolutionary viewpoint and the scriptural expression combined with contemporary psychological insights about the development of person and human self-actualization begin to provide us with some plausible answer to some of our initial questions regarding human fulfillment and the Christian faith. All dichotomies break down in Christ. If we ask whether one can be a fully contemporary person and a son or daughter of God we can now look at Jesus in all of his human relationships and answer positively. Jesus was more deeply immersed in the human and in the world than any one who ever lived. At one and the same time, he found his fundamental mutuality in relationship to the One he named Abba. This extraordinary single-mindedness of his mutuality with God is lived out in his human relationships. "My mother and my brothers—they are those who hear the word of God and act upon it." This is not a negation of physical relationships or human sexuality, but a transcendence and a transignification that is a paradigm in itself. Human relationships, when they are truly human, personalized, and self-transcending, are revelatory of the Ultimate. A Christian anthropology, a Creation theology, that looks at Jesus relationally, suggests that the only way of becoming more human, more person, more who we are called to be, is to be in relationship both with the one called Abba, the Mystery of Life, and with each other as we live our own mystery.

---

[6]Teilhard de Chardin, "The Sense of Man," *Towards the Future,* 34.

Conclusion

Towards a Contemporary Creation Spirituality

In Christ, *God chose us* before the world was founded, to
be dedicated, to be without blemish in God's sight, *to be full
of love*.... God has made known God's own hidden purpose ... to be put into effect when the time was ripe:
namely, that the universe all in heaven and earth, might be
brought into a *unity* in Christ.

Eph. 1:4,9-10

Our earth is but a small star in the great universe, yet of it
we can make, if we choose, a planet unvexed by war, un-
troubled by hunger or fear, undivided by senseless distinctions of race, color or theory.

Stephen Vincent Benet

Two sources of reflection on creation in the universe and its mysterious meaning in divine/human terms ... each emphasize again the relationships that we have been pondering and the framework against which we have looked at them ... the Ultimate Mystery that we have named God, humanity, earth, the universe, and the Christ. Just as soon as we acknowledge that God's created universe can only be spoken of in the category of on-going process, everything flowing from it must be seen in that light as well. Science and lived experience do not stand to contradict religious belief, but they do demand that religious discourse make some dramatic semantic shifts in order to be authentic and intelligible. So, in a universe where natural physical catastrophes and cataclysms have been and are expectable, and where human frailty and moral immaturity are commonplace, questions about our own concepts of God, God's relatedness to the human, and "dependence" on human growth and fulfillment to accomplish God's design must find new expression.

The Pauline language in the passage above, from Ephesians, is that of choice—God chose *us,* the human community, before there was a world, to become and embody all these loving qualities which we have usually reserved for Christ. But there is no doubt or ambiguity in Paul's text that *in* Christ, *the* Human, God chose *humanity* to be full of Love, to live the human/divine life, to be dedicated, as was the Christ, to bringing about unity in the whole of the universe, when the time would be ripe. Stephen Vincent Benet's poetic challenge is also about choice—the choices we make to bring about unity on planet earth. He suggests that the time is ripe. The earth is a tiny star. It is not the center of the universe. It *is* "manageable," in terms of taking care of the poor and hungry; it is possible to teach peace-making; we have developed enough self-knowledge and self-consciousness to understand that divisions and antipathies based on race, color, ideology, religion, and gender are truly senseless. But, we must choose to act on this evolved self-consciousness and knowledge. We have come a long way towards seeing that the "spiritual journey" is the human drama played out in the flesh and blood that is one throughout the planet. Creation, incarnation, redemption, resurrection, a world in process of transformation— these are all processes co-extensive in time and duration, not sequential or in any way separate. If, indeed, we have arrived at the point of evolution when the time is ripe for us to seize the situation and change the face of the earth, it is *because* creation, redemption and resurrection endure in space/time, constantly calling humanity forward to change. The raising up of the humanity of Jesus of Nazareth to fill the earth with his Spirit, God's Spirit, symbolizes the continued raising of all humanity. Each time that we overcome something which stands in the way of accomplishing God's great work of unifying, of convergence, of building the Whole, we move closer to the moment when the Mystery that we so little comprehend shall be All in All. Albert Einstein struggled to find a "simple principle," believing that nature itself is simple and beautiful, and, as Leonard Bernstein had his protagonist in the opera "Mass" sing: "God is the simplest of all." The movement from the multiple to the one is constant.

One of the faces of created reality that seeks greater unity and integration as we have examined it, is the absolute and essential role of the feminine. Masculine attitudes about being have held too much pre-eminence, been too isolated. The feminine dimension of reality impresses itself upon human consciousness more surely and strongly than ever before. The most basic movement towards union, the sexual, must be enlarged and seen as convergence of the whole person, of eros and agape, with a deepened sense of appreciation and respect for all that woman brings to the union *beyond* physical fecundity. In the same movement, the ability of men and women to come together in union for reasons other than sexual intimacy must be seen as absolutely essential to the accomplishment of the tremendous tasks at hand. The fecundity and nurturing of the feminine principle must be found in collaborative efforts at creative politics, creative liturgy, creative art forms, concern for the environment and all questions about living beings. Collaborative common effort that is warm and caring, noncompetitive, leading to genuine empathy and friendship, is crucial to the work of creative redemption and redemptive creation.

The emphasis that has been placed on human responsibility and deliberate, positive action does not overlook the message of the Cross. Rather it sees the Cross as sign and symbol of the very structure of life. The upward vertical bar is constantly countered by the horizontal cross bar, the struggle to move through and over evil, suffering, pain and death to fuller, newer life. The Cross and suffering have no meaning except in light of the risen life—the life of transformation and continued quest. The quest is *to be full of love*. But while we are still in process, that means that we are actively trying to learn to love authentically, to integrate our person into communities of love and communities where there is no love. The quest is to discover creative means to see that human dignity is furthered in every corner, that personal liberation becomes reality, that truth and justice are done, not just talked about. In our quest, we must seek to move from a competitive stance to a sharing stance, from a fear of "the world" to a love of earth, from a mistrust of the senses to a trust in the mysteries of human experience. The quest searches out ways to recapture the beauty of fidelity and commitment in the midst of irresponsible risk, risking to speak God's word. What then can we say about a truly human and contemporary spirituality? A truly human contemporary spirituality will be aware of, open to, and interdependent with the whole world, aware of the continued presence of Transcendence in our midst, despite the vast mysteries of the universe, and aware of the presence of Transcendence in the whole of the human community, despite the seeming differences of the diverse communities.

What once, in other ages, may have suggested withdrawal from the world for development of spirituality, can no longer be understood in that way once we have affirmed the unity of all matter and spirit, the relatedness of all things. Disdain for the world, fear of its being destroyed by a vindictive God— any negative dimension which marked a former eschatological view—is distinctly out of place in a spirituality which calls for a personal and united human effort to become who we are called to be. And so, in our search for *Person,* our own and that of others, we are not looking for the development of "individuality" in the sense of the selfish interest which grips so many in today's culture, but for situations and relationships in which personality, rather than individuality, can flourish. We cannot expect persons who have become so aware of change and personal development as being of prime value to regard institutional, social or national situations that are closed or exclusive with any degree of approval. The "community" that the liberated person will seek will be marked by a spirit of searching inquiry, by a spirit of ecumenism, flexibility, autonomy, the gift for calling forth the best in everyone, and the giving of the best to all.

But this kind of human community cannot *ultimately* be created by ourselves alone. The love we seek is neither you nor I, but the love that exists between us. Benet's assurance that we can choose to make our star a better place needs the added dimension of a Center that will hold.

As we move toward each other, healing and reconciling, trying to make Whole, we need to remember that the Love which is the bond of union, the Center upon whom all loves converge is both immanent in ourselves and transcendent of all that we are. The words that we speak to one another are not themselves the sealing bond, but they are rooted in a cosmic Word of promise meant for all humanity, the Word of Hope, the Word of God.

That hope and that promise—that we can all become who we are called to be, that we can at last be simply ourselves—is held out in a most beautiful sacred symbol in the mysterious last book of Scripture. As we began with God speaking Creation, we can close with an intriguing word that sends us on a search. Let whoever has ears to hear, hear the word of the quest. It is only a metaphor; it doesn't say all that there is to say, but it has long been one of my favorite passages. It speaks to each of us in the human family, existing as dyad, male and female, for our search can never take place in isolation, no matter how splendid isolation may seem. But if it is completed, if we do become whole, full of love, ourselves, surely that is a translation of the writer of Revelation's "victorious." The search will have fulfilled its meaning. This is the promise held out to the whole of creation.

> To the ones who are 'victorious,' I will give a white stone, upon which will be inscribed a new and hidden name, known only to the one who receives it.
>
> Revelation 2:17

Called into becoming, yearning to know our own true name, humanity is drawn to an unknown future, in hope, in spite of the destructive forces that would hem us in. Our "new spirituality" will be one that takes all the earth and our own body/ spirit with live seriousness.

The great concerns of the earth today revolve around tremendous human issues. Christian spirituality, as it evolves in its understanding of Christ as permeating all reality, will address itself to the human project as being central to all prayer and living. Compassion becomes the new/old watchword. The next "logical" step for humanity is to become loving. The ruptured, aching, pain-filled world cannot be the occasion for despair, cynicism or talk of God's death. It must become the occasion for pouring oil, breaking bread, sharing wine, binding wounds, healing grievances. It is the occasion for reintroducing the arts, music, and poetry into the structures of life from beginning to end, as being necessary elements for humanization.

I would like to recall the process language that has been employed, in order to invite reflection on these thematic words: freeing, reconciling, creative, imaginative, redemptive, relational, personal, communal, vulnerable, celebrative, ecstatic, integral, dynamic and cosmic. These are basically "biblical," scriptural words, words about humanity and God's word in human forms. They are, like scripture, poetic and symbolic, and therefore, able to speak to all of us, women and men, young and old. They bespeak the yearning that we have to step out of ourselves ecstatically, to be free, to be whole. Precisely because we are called to the fullness expressed in these creative/redemptive motifs, we are painfully aware of the obstacles which make the eschatological expectation seem to be always just out of reach.

> But to see is no longer to hope: why should one endure and wait for what one already sees? But if we hope for something we do not yet see, then in waiting for it, we show our endurance.
>
> Rom 8:24-25

It would seem that one of the contributions a contemporary theology of creation and spirituality might make to this question of "waiting while we do not see clearly" is to remove any idea that endurance need be passive resignation, a waiting on "God's will," without realizing that if God is mutual with the world, we must act—in Bonhoeffer's oft-quoted phrase—"as if God were not." The initiative is God's, the instrumentality, ours.

Faith in God *and* the world become faith and hope in God *through* the world. A contemporary spirituality will thus be open to the world and to the future, changing constantly, finding the beginning of heaven in a life lived for and with others. A contemporary Christian, believing in the world and loving the humanity of Jesus, can trust the future to the cosmic Christ, who holds in store for humanity what eye has not seen and, at the same time, can act to bring about that future. For Christ holds out that promise from his vantage point as Christ-Omega. Having achieved the fullness of humanity, and so received his own new and hidden name, he waits to reveal ours—and not only the names of all who are human, but the names, the very meaning of all that has been created.

In a magnificent, mystical understanding of this cosmic naming, and "selfing" phenomenon, the English poet Gerard Manley Hopkins gives us a fitting epilogue to these reflections on a world in the process of being created and transformed, in which everything that is, is filled with Spirit, is unique, and unrepeatable, and in which the mystery of the Christ and creation in Christ become co-extensive with the cosmos.

EPILOGUE

As kingfishers catch fire, dragonflies draw flame;
As tumbled over rim in roundy wells
Stones ring; like each tucked string tells, each hung bell's
Bow swung finds tongue to fling out broad its name;
Each mortal thing does one thing and the same:
Deals out that being indoors each one dwells;
Selves—goes itself; myself it speaks and spells;
Crying; What I do is me: for that I came.

I say more: the just man justices;
Keeps grace: that keeps all his goings graces;
Acts in God's eyes what in God's eyes he is—
Christ—for Christ plays in ten thousand places,
Lovely in limbs, and lovely in eyes not his
To the Father, through the features of men's faces.

Gerard Manley Hopkins

Selected Bibliography

Following is a brief bibliography of books and articles germane to the concept of this book:

Berry, Thomas, "Building the Earth," *Riverdale Papers II,* New York: Riverdale Center, 1979.

Bok, Sissela, *A Strategy For Peace: Human Values and the Threat of War,* New York: Pantheon Books, 1989.

Donders, Joseph, *The Global Believer,* Mystic, CT: Twenty-third Publications, 1986.

Ferguson, Marilyn, *Aquarian Conspiracy: Personal and Social Transformation in the 1980's,* Los Angeles: J. F. Torcher, 1980.

Fiorenza, Elisabeth Schüssler, *In Memory of Her: A Feminist Reconstruction of Christian Origins,* New York: Crossroads, 1983.

Jastrow, Robert, *God and the Astronomers,* New York: Warner Books, 1978.

Lash, Nicholas and David Tracy, eds., *Cosmology and Theology,* New York: Seabury Press, 1983.

Moltmann, Jurgen, *God in Creation: A New Theology of Creation and the Spirit of God,* San Francisco: Harper and Row, 1985.

North, Robert, *In Search of the Human Jesus,* Washington, DC: Corpus, 1970, 6, 14.

Schillebeeckx, Edward, *God is New Each Moment,* tr. D. Smith, New York: Seabury Press, 1983.

Schoonenberg, Piet, *God's World in the Making,* Techny, IL: Divine Word Publications, 1968.

Simon, Arthur, *Bread for the World,* Englewood, NJ: Paulist Press, 1985

Soelle, Dorothee, *To Work and to Love: A Theology of Creation,* Philadelphia, PA: Fortress Press, 1984.

Teilhard de Chardin, Pierre, *The Phenomenon of Man* tr. B. Wall, revised translation, New York: Harper and Row, 1965.

——————, *The Future of Man,* tr. N. Denny, New York: Harper and Row, 1947.

——————, *Towards the Future,* tr. R. Hague, New York: Harcourt, Brace, Jovanovich, 1975.

——————, *Science and Christ,* tr. R. Hague, New York: Harper and Row, 1968.

——————, *Christianity and Evolution,* New York: Harcourt, Brace, Jovanovich, 1969.

——————, "Le Christ Evoluteur," *Cahiers de la Fondation Teilhard de Chardin,* 5, Paris; Editions du Seuil, 1963.

Trible, Phyllis, *God and the Rhetoric of Sexuality* (Overtures to Biblical Theology 2), Philadelphia, PA: Fortress Press, 1978.

Von Rad, Gerhard, *Theological Dictionary of the New Testament,* ed. G. Kittel, Grand Rapids: Eerdmans, 1964, 152, 165.

Walker, Alice, *The Color Purple,* New York, Washington Square Press, 1982, 175-179.

Periodicals

Balducelli, Roger, "Decision for Celibacy," *Theological Studies* 36, 1975, 236.

Berry, Thomas, "Perspectives on Creativity: Openness to a

Free Future," *Whither Creativity, Freedom, Suffering?: Humanity, Cosmos, God,* ed. Francis Eigo, OSA, Villanova, PA: Villanova University Press, 1981, 1-24.

Binns, Emily, "Defining Humanity in Every Age: The Christ Event as Paradigm," *Whither Creativity, Freedom, Suffering?: Humanity, Cosmos, God,* ed. Francis Eigo, OSA, Villanova, PA: Villanova University Press 1981, 77-104.

Buchanan, James, "Creation and Cosmos: The Symbolics of Proclamation and Participation," *Cosmology and Theology,* ed, Nicholas Lash and David Tracy, New York: Seabury Press, 1983, 37-43.

Buck, Harry M., "Creation Stories and Creation Science," *Anima* 8, Spring 1982, 34-42.

Dwyer, John "Theoretical Linguistics and the Problems of Christology,"*Catholic Theological Proceedings* 42, 1987, 16, passim.

Floyd, Wayne, "Christ, Concreteness, and Creation in the Early Bonhoeffer," *Union Seminary Quarterly Review* 39, no. 1, 1984, 104-114.

Gilkey, Langdon, "The Creationist Issue: A Theologian's View," *Cosmology and Theology,* ed. Nicholas Lash and David Tracy, New York: Seabury Press, 1983.

Granberg-Michaelson, "Earthkeeping: A Theology of Global Sanctification," *Sojourners* II, October 1982, 21-24.

Gray, Donald, "Creative Convergence" *Anima* 7, Spring 1981, 110-113.

Hesse, Mary, "Cosmology as Myth," *Cosmology and Theology,* ed. Nicholas Lash and David Tracy, New York: Seabury Press, 1983.

Mooney, Christopher, "Survival: Teilhard and an Unlimited Future," *Chicago Studies,* 207-220.

Pabee, John S., "Creation, Faith and Responsibility for the

World," *Journal of the Theology Society for Africa* 50, March 1985, 15-28.

Tshibangu, Tshishiku, "Eschatology and Cosmology," *Cosmology and Theology,* ed. Nicholas Lash and David Tracy, New York: Seabury Press, 1983.

Church Documents

"Gaudium et Spes," *Documents of Vatican II,* New York: Guild Press, 1961.

"Humani Generis," 1950, Pius XII (NCWC translation).

The Teaching of the Catholic Church (as contained in her documents), ed. Karl Rahner, S.J. (originally Joseph Neuner, S.J. and Heinrich Roos, S.J.), New York: Mercier Press, Ltd., 1967.

The Anti-Pelagian Works of St. Augustine, V. II,III (trans. Peter Holmes), Edinburgh: T & T Clark 1874.

Appendices

The attached appendices are provided to give some chrono-logy of specific theological and scientific developments spoken about within the text. In each instance, they must be seen against a backdrop of developing human understanding, as this has been seen in biblical studies, anthropology, and con-temporary science.

Appendix 1: Traditional Church Doctrine on Creation and Original Sin

The traditional teachings of the Church on creation and ori-ginal sin may be articulated in the following propositions, with at least one reference to a Church Council or high level church document for each proposition. These have been collected in *The Teaching of the Catholic Church,* ed Neuner-Roos. (The numeration refers to NR.)

1. God created the whole world out of nothing. (C. of Florence, a.d. 1442, NR 177.)

2. God created the world from the beginning of time. (Vat. I, a.d. 1870, NR 191.)

3. God created the human species and the entire material world. (Vat. I, NR 197.)

4. All creation, including matter, is good. (4th Lateran C. a.d. 1215, NR 171.)

5. The human soul is the form of the body. (C. Vienne, a.d. 1311, NR 203.)

6. The first man was given the gift of sanctifying grace as a free gift of God, not due to his human nature. (C. Trent, A.D. 1540. NR 221.)

7. The first man was not subject to death. (5th Latern V. A.D. 1513. NR 205.)

8. Adam sinned and this sin of Adam affects all his descendants. (C. Trent, a.d. 1545-63, NR 223-225).

9. By his sin Adam forfeited his supernatural gifts of immortality and sanctifying grace. (C. Trent, NR 221, 222.)

10. Original sin is overcome in the Sacrament of the Baptism by reparation made by Christ. (C. Trent, NR 223-225.)

The question of the evolution of the human body is an open one. The encyclical *Humani Genesis* (1950) by Pope Pius XII was an important milestone in the official teaching of the Church concerning evolution. In 1941 the Pope had declared that the question of the association of man with the animal kingdom, so far as his body is concerned, is an open one. Then, in the encyclical mentioned, the pontiff, reflecting on the consensus of the teaching church, again declared freedom in discussing the evolution of the human body. (NR 205.)

Not all of the above references to the teaching of the Church have equal weight, and each text of a council or magisterial document needs to be evaluated and understood in the context of the intention of the authors, and the context of the time and situation in which the document was promulgated, much in the manner that particular scriptural texts are evaluated and interpreted.

The above propositions undoubtedly throw much light on the various historical phases of progressing and maturing thought the human race has been through. However, the search for ever clearer theological understanding of our origins have obviously gone beyond the above propositions and the issues behind them. Quite often, the very questions we ask today about the origins of the universe and all that is in it have changed. For example, we are not so much concerned today about whether God created the universe or not, but rather *how* God, in His infinite wisdom and resourcefulness, used the laws of the cosmos and of biological evolution to bring about the human species on our planet earth as we know them.

Appendix 2: *Chronology of Philosophical and Scientific Understandings*

The philosophical and scientific understandings of creation have likewise undergone incredible change through the centuries. Scientists and philosophers have presented multiple understandings of planet earth and the solar system. For example, in 340 B.C., ARISTOTLE, in his book "On the Heavens," put forth arguments for the earth's being a sphere. However, along with most of his contemporaries, he thought that the earth was the "center" of the universe and "eternal".

In the 2nd century B.C., PTOLEMY also held for a geocentric universe, but with the addition of an accurate system for predicting positions of heavenly bodies that remained for centuries until the time of Galileo.

COPERNICUS (1514) proposed another model of the cosmos, with the *sun* as the center. GALILEO later supported Copernicus, with experimental data dealing a death blow to prior geocentric theories. GALILEO was a turning point in human speculation about the cosmos. The predominant system of thought in the 16th century was Aristotle (largely because of) the commentaries of St. Thomas Aquinas. But Galileo boldly opposed Aristotle and Ptolemy, agreeing with Copernicus.

While Galileo was supported by the prominent Jesuit astronomer and mathematician, Christopher Clavius of the Roman College, he was opposed by prominent churchmen, including no less than the most famous and respected theologian of the time, Cardinal Robert Bellarmine.

Bellarmine's views and power prevailed and in 1616, under the chairmanship of Bellarmine, a papal commission banned the principal work of Copernicus, which Galileo so staunchly defended. In 1633, at the age of 70, Galileo was summoned to Rome. There he was put on trial by papal commission for this defense of Copernicus. His own book "Dialogue" was banned, a ban not to be lifted until 1822. He was forced to abjure the Copernican opinion. He spent the last years of his life under house arrest in Florence, writing and working despite the loss of his sight.

In 1687, ISAAC NEWTON elaborated the law of universal gravitation, according to which each heavenly body is attracted to every other heavenly body, a phenomenon obvious enough when we drop something from a height, but not so obvious when applied to stars that are light-years away.

In 1929 EDWIN HUBBLE, who had already discovered and measured the movements of galaxies other than our own, made the observation, which was to prove monumental, that the entire universe is expanding. Each heavenly body is moving away from every other heavenly body. There was a "time," according to Hubble, called the "Big Bang," when the universe was very small but infinitely dense, and suddenly explosively began to expand. This is the "beginning of time."

The question about whether the universe began in time or in eternity is an old one, which antedates modern astronomy. Aristotle, as we have seen, held that the cosmos is eternal. St. Thomas Aquinas said it could be. There is, of course, no inherent incompatibility philosophically between a created and an eternal universe. If matter existed in any state before the "Big Bang", that matter, no matter how dense and as yet unstructured still needed as a maker, or to use the Aristo-telian-Thomistic terms, a First Cause, or an Unmoved Mover, outside of time. Philosophical discussion on this interesting point will undoubtedly continue for a long time to come. Meantime, astronomers and mathematicians talk about an infinitely small and infinitely dense pre-big-bang universe for which time has no meaning, since time is the measure of motion of particles which had not yet begun to move.

Contemporary astro-physicists described the universe in terms of two basic theories: (1) The General Theory of Relativity, attributed mostly to Albert Einstein (1915), and (2) Quantum Mechanics, initiated and pioneered about 1900 by Max Planck. These theories, while incomplete and still being refined, are acclaimed as among the greatest intellectual break-throughs in the first half of this century. The theory of relativity deals with large-scale forces in the universe. Quantum mech-anics deals with phenomena in the universe of extremely small scale. All scientific efforts today in the search for meaning of the universe assume the validity of these theories. While they throw much light on the laws of energy and all the time/space issues, they have enlarged the issues and multiplied the questions.

Quantum mechanics assumes the elements of unpredictability in recent theorizing about the origin and fate of the universe. It is interesting to note that Einstein, who was awarded a Nobel prize for his contribution to Quantum Mechanics, never accepted the proposition that the universe was controlled by chance. "God doesn't play dice" was his now-famous remark in response to the idea that chance governs the universe.

Relativity Theory (Albert Einstein) maintains the absence of any fixed point against which to measure motion anywhere in the universe. All movement is relative to something else taken as non-moving (e.g. we measure the speed of an automobile against the "motionless" road, but the road is also moving with the planet and the planet with the solar system and the solar system with the galaxy etc.) Constitutive of Einstein's relativity theory is the absence of any cosmos pervading material (classically called "ether"), in which things, gravity or light, move. Light is involved in the matter-energy conversion and its speed is a constant in nature (Hence: E (energy) = M (matter) x C^2 (speed of light squared).

Quantum Theory holds that energy, like matter, comes in the smallest, most discrete packets, and that energetic particles cannot occupy random positions in the continuum of space, but discrete positions relative to one another. (e.g. atoms cannot spontaneously collapse by a cascade of electrons into the nucleus).

Uncertainty Principle (Werner Heisenberg) states that any measurement (a quantization) disturbs the object measured and perturbs another parameter of the object (e.g. to measure a particle's speed one necessarily modifies its location). One simply cannot know all about anything.

The widespread acceptance of quantum mechanics has been due mostly to the fact that, as a theoretical system, it explains with amazing accuracy what has happened and is happening to the universe.

The greatest possible tribute to quantum mechanics is that, as a giant hypothesis that has been tested by scientific observations over and over again, it lies at the bottom of nearly all successful technology today in the field of electronics. Quantum mechanics is behind the behaviors and productive use of transistors and integrated circuits from which T.V. sets and amazingly versatile computers are made and interconnected globally.

Appendix 3: Condemnations of Heretical Positions

Condemnation of the Pelagians:

Pelagius and the Pelagians were condemned by the
C. of Carthage, a.d. 418 (NR 224)
Also by the *2nd C. of Orange,* a.d. 529 (NR 206, 220)

Condemnation of the Manicheans:

C. of Constantinople a.d. 543
C. of Braga (Portugal) a.d. 581
4th Lateran C. a.d. 1215
C. Florence a.d. 1442
C. Vat I a.d. 1870

Condemnation of the Jansenists:

Errors of Cornelius Jansen cond'd by P. Innocent X, a.d. 1653, (NR 790-794)
Jansenists Errors cond'd: by P. Alexander VIII a.d. 1690, (NR 324)

Index

Subject Index